SOMEWHERE
ALONG THE WAY

A 600 mile journey on
the Camino De Santiago

Jordan P. Jones

Copyright © 2020 Jordan P. Jones.

All rights reserved. No part of this book may be reproduced, stored, or transmitted by any means—whether auditory, graphic, mechanical, or electronic—without written permission of the author, except in the case of brief excerpts used in critical articles and reviews. Unauthorized reproduction of any part of this work is illegal and is punishable by law.

Because of the dynamic nature of the Internet, any web addresses or links contained in this book may have changed since publication and may no longer be valid. The views expressed in this work are solely those of the author and do not necessarily reflect the views of the publisher, and the publisher hereby disclaims any responsibility for them.

Any people depicted in stock imagery provided by Getty Images are models, and such images are being used for illustrative purposes only. Certain stock imagery © Getty Images.

Interior Image Credit: Jordan Philip Jones, Marc Geboers

ISBN: 978-1-7164-5095-2 (sc)
ISBN: 978-1-7164-5097-6 (hc)
ISBN: 978-1-7164-5094-5 (e)

Library of Congress Control Number: 2020923439

Lulu Publishing Services rev. date: 12/30/2020

*Dedicated to my mother Jill, my father Philip and my nan Joyce
for raising me with the courage, strength and determination I need
to travel the world
alone
xxx*

*Sadly, my nan Joyce died while I was writing this book. She died
peacefully in her sleep on Sunday 17th November 2019, aged 94.
It makes me sad she'll never get to read this, but
I hope it would have made her proud*

For every pilgrim that has ever walked to Santiago

In loving memory of Nigel Baker and Betsie Geboers

Travelling.

It leaves you speechless,
then turns you
into a
storyteller.

Introduction

I first heard of the Camino back in 2012, after watching a documentary on the internet. A solo male traveller, with a camera attached to his head, walked the Camino while giving his own commentary. I was instantly drawn to it by the distance people covered every day and the sense of freedom that would come with it. I loved seeing how these pilgrims would just wake up every morning in a different town or city and walk further and further each day across Spain. I had travelled alone around Europe in the previous few years but nothing on this scale, I had never walked the length of a country before. That was one of the main attractions for me – to be able to say I've walked across the largest country in Western Europe. Not many people can say they've achieved something like that.

My first Camino was planned for 2013, with flights booked and everything planned out, but due to work commitments I had to cancel. I was extremely disappointed, and being in work while knowing I should have been on the Camino was devastating for weeks. I would read the Camino blogs on the internet and feel like I was missing out on something amazing, but I knew it wouldn't be long until I was there myself, being a pilgrim.

It was during that time of devastation that I planned my next trip, for July 2015. I remember going into work and saying these exact words to my boss: 'I know I haven't been here long, but in July 2015 I'm doing the Camino de Santiago. I will need about six weeks off work. I can appreciate that's a long time, but it's booked and something I need to do. Hopefully we can work something out that doesn't affect my job or the company.' That's how determined I was to do the Camino. If it had come to July 2015 and I couldn't get the time off work I would have quit my job, no doubt about it. I was lucky that over the two years leading up to the Camino, I got to become very good friends with my boss and was given as much time as I needed to complete The Way.

I'd read about people becoming 'hooked' on the Camino, finding themselves thinking about it constantly in the months leading up to the start date, and it was no different for me. I would constantly daydream about walking over hills, mountains or through small Spanish streets, until it became annoying. For the next two years I worked and saved, while still daydreaming of the Camino, and before I knew it 2015 was upon me and it was time to go.

The day before leaving I was excited for what the Camino had in store for me and I couldn't wait to get started. A lot of people I later met on the Camino told me about being scared and nervous in the days leading up to the start, but it was a totally different feeling for me. Travelling alone has never scared me and I think of it as an adventure, something I prefer to do alone. Maybe my feelings will change when I'm older, but I hope not.

At the time I worked in the security industry and the shifts were very long. The day before I left for the Camino, I was working a fifteen-hour shift and I couldn't concentrate on anything; I was just full of excitement. I finally finished work at 8pm, with my plane leaving Heathrow at 12:30 the next morning.

Now it is real, I thought to myself. *I'm leaving in just a matter of hours.*

I woke up at 4am. My parents were giving me a lift to Cardiff bus station and from there I would take a bus to London Heathrow for my flight to France. My mother and father usually drop me at this bus station whenever I go travelling and are used to me just packing a bag and going somewhere at the drop of a hat. My mother used to get really upset whenever I went away for a long time, and I thought she was used to it by now, but she obviously wasn't, as she was crying as I walked away to get on the bus. I was twenty-six and could look after myself more than enough, but she still thought I was going to die, or else perhaps she'd never see me again. My father is the same, but he never shows it. My brother and sister are both older than me but have never travelled to the extent I have; they go on holidays with their families, but nothing more. My parents had never had to deal with one of their kids leaving for a long time before, then I came along and jump on a plane as fast as I possibly can. I even moved from Wales to the north of England for three years and didn't see them all that much, but I don't think they will ever get used to it, really.

The bus left Cardiff at 6am and would get to the airport around 10:30, given everything went to plan. I crossed my fingers and thankfully it did. The bus ride from Cardiff to London isn't particularly nice, so I decided to get my head down to make the journey go faster

I got to the airport on time and while there I looked around to see if I could notice any backpacks with Camino patches on them, but I didn't see any. Actually, nobody on my flight looked like they were about to walk across a country.

The Camino

The bus got into Heathrow at 10:20 and I was in plenty of time, so I checked in and waited for the plane. Heathrow was its usual busy self, but I love the airport. I like to look around and wonder where people are going and for what reason. Millions of people every single day flying all over the world, it's amazing. I was flying to Biarritz and then getting a train to Bayonne, where I'd then get a bus to Saint-Jean-Pied-de-Port to start the walk.

Getting off the plane in Biarritz was heaven; walking out onto the runway and feeling the heat smack you straight in the face is something I always love. The train to Bayonne and bus to Saint-Jean flew by. I was too excited thinking about the Camino and talking to other pilgrims I met on the bus. The bus stopped in Saint-Jean and I didn't have a clue where to go, but luckily enough a helpful restaurant owner pointed me in the right direction. I followed another pilgrim up a very steep shortcut, next to the side of a church, and found myself looking down at the main, cobbled street of Saint-Jean-Pied-de-Port.

I wrote the following in my journal…

'So, I'm in Saint-Jean. The place is stunning, very little, but full of life. I'm amazed by how many pilgrims are here and wonder how many of these people I will talk to or become friends with over the next 600 miles of walking. Every shop in Saint-Jean's main street seems to be selling clothes, bags, walking poles or something else related to the Camino. The streets are long and narrow, and nearly every building is painted white, with red beams on the outside, just like you would imagine a small town in France. It looks typically French.'

After writing in my journal, I wanted to drop my bag off somewhere, so I decided to look for a hotel or an albergue. I found an albergue at the top of town, next to the famous St James' Gate and Bridiers Castle. For the life of me I can't remember the name of the albergue, but I remember there were around forty beds, split between two rooms. The bed didn't come with breakfast but was still a good price. When I was on the bus from Bayonne to Saint-Jean, I met a girl from London who was also walking the Camino. We didn't get each other's names, but she was very nice and happened to be staying in the same albergue that night. The room I was in was small, with bunkbeds crammed together like sardines, and not the cleanest of places. But for eight euros, it was worth it.

I was on the top bunk and below me was a man from Gibraltar who kindly let me use the shower before him. It was his second Camino, but his first one alone, and he was eager to make friends. After my shower I got dressed in some comfortable clothes and decided to explore Saint-Jean. I was going to ask my new friend from Gibraltar if he wanted a beer, but he ended up leaving while I was showering.

Saint-Jean-Pied-de-Port literally means 'St John at the foot of the pass', and is the last town you can enter before you tackle the very steep, very hot Pyrenees mountains and cross the border into Spain. The steep, cobbled, narrow main street of Saint-Jean is burrowed in between 300-400-year-old buildings on either side and is so charming to see. Most of the buildings here still have the original features and inscriptions over the doors. I love seeing things like that.

At the very bottom of the hill is the stunning Gothic church, Notre-Dame-du-Bout-du-Pont. I stayed in here a while admiring the big, colourful windows that portray Jesus on the cross and lit a candle for those back home, hoping it would keep them safe while I was away.

The main river running through Saint-Jean was really peaceful as I sat on a bench with a beer just staring at the water for over an hour. I was due to start walking in the morning and had all sorts of things running through my mind.

I really started to doubt myself, and that's not like me. I was starting to think I was stupid and that I couldn't walk 600 miles across a country. I mean, when you think of it like that – 'I'm about to start WALKING across a whole country' – it's extremely daunting. The most exciting, nervous, amazing feeling I have ever had, but so daunting.

There's only so much of Saint-Jean you can see and I'd pretty much gazed upon everything after three hours of walking around. I decided to try out some of the local food but was surprised by how many of the restaurants only sold English/American style food. The restaurants on basically 70%percent of the Camino are made for tourists, so you have to do a bit of searching to find a local menu. I ended up settling for a hamburger and fries, which I was reluctant to enjoy. Part of travelling is enjoying local food and discovering tastes you've never tried before, but the Camino is commercial these days and sadly most menus are just like back home (if home is Europe or the U.S.).

After food I decided to walk back up the cobbled, sloped hill and go back to the albergue to meet some of my follow pilgrims, and maybe find a walking buddy to start the day with the next day. When I arrived back, there were four or five pilgrims sitting outside in the garden, talking and drinking wine. I said no to the wine but yes to joining in the chat, as I didn't want to start my first day walking with a hangover. I didn't like wine much, anyway, but that would change during my Camino. I spoke to a lovely Canadian woman in her sixties called Jennifer, who told me she'd been married for thirty-two years and this was her first time abroad without her husband. She got quite upset talking about him and started to cry. I got the feeling he didn't like her being alone on the Camino and they'd had some sort of falling out over it before she left. I never saw Jennifer again after that night, but I got to realise in our three hours of talking how important the Camino was for her, and I hope she had the time of her life. I wish I could have had more time with her on the road, but it wasn't meant to be. I think I learned my first lesson that night on the Camino, when she told me this before going to bed…

'I'm a lot older than you, Jordan, and I want you to listen to my advice. No matter how difficult something is, you must follow your dreams and do what you want to do. Nobody can live forever, and this is my last chance to do the Camino, because time isn't waiting for me. Yes, I'll miss my family, but when I'm on my deathbed I don't want to look back and feel like I've missed out. Don't live your life for other people; make yourself happy.'

A few hours later, I thought about that before going to sleep. I realised that she was in her sixties and this was her last chance to do anything like this before she got too old. I, on the other hand, was in my late twenties, with my whole life in front of me. I'd never thought about life catching up with me and being too old to do things I've always wanted; I'd taken it for granted, and that made me realise that nothing should be taken for granted. Life would catch up with me soon and I'd be saying the same thing to a guy in his late twenties.

The lesson: Don't wait. If you want to do something, go do it.

Everyone in the albergue was in bed by 9pm, the lights were off and the albergue door was locked, but sleeping wasn't on anyone's mind. We were all anticipating the climb over the Pyrenees in the morning, and you could sense everyone's excitement as they whispered and laughed like children. Soon enough everyone fell asleep, but I was left wide awake. I've seen on countless documentaries people complaining about the snoring of other pilgrims in the night and thought to myself, 'I'll be OK, I'll just use earplugs or else be so tired from walking I'll fall straight asleep.' How wrong was I. These rooms are small, with many beds packed in, and you can hear EVERYTHING! I was on a top bunk and the guy below me was snoring like something I'd never heard before. My father is the loudest snorer I've ever heard, but this guy beat him tenfold. I looked around the room and everybody was sleeping. It was just my luck to be on top of the only snorer in the room. I lay there for around two hours, listening to my music with headphones in, then managed to drop off to sleep around 12:30.

At 5am people were starting to wake up and get themselves ready for the first day, probably the hardest day of the entire walk. I decided to do the same, even though I hadn't had much sleep. The bustle every morning is so loud you have no choice but to wake up with your fellow pilgrims.

The first day of walking is over the French Pyrenees and takes around seven to nine hours to complete, while climbing to around 1,450 metres above sea level. It is tough, believe me! You cross the border into Spain on these mountains (there's a sign in the middle of nowhere telling you when you've crossed).

Before I went anywhere, I had to wait for the Pilgrim Office to open to receive my map and pilgrim passport. The pilgrim passport is a white fold-out card that you must get stamped at every town you pass through, or every albergue you stay at. This proves that you are walking the Camino and at the end entitles you to a Compostela (a certificate written in Latin to confirm that you have walked the Camino de Santiago). The Pilgrim Office didn't open until 8am and was very busy with people collecting their passports. I should have gone the day before and sorted it out, but I wanted to explore. That's the traveller in me, I suppose. A lovely old Spanish gentleman working in the Pilgrim Office handed me my passport and told me he had three tips to share with me on walking the Camino.

1. Take care of your feet and they will take care of you.
2. It gets hard, but do not give up. It will be worth it in the end.
3. Love is free. Give it and accept it.

Those three tips would stay with me my whole Camino and helped me so much at times. If someone asks me for tips on the Camino, I tell them the same three things.

They are all you need to hear.

I didn't get walking until around 9am and knew I wouldn't get to Roncesvalles (the first town after you cross the Pyrenees) until after 4pm. I was fine with this but knew the pilgrims that left before me would get beds. I became worried there would be none left when I got there, but I decided to start walking anyway and stop worrying so much. What will be, will be.

The walk to begin with shocked me. As soon as you leave Saint-Jean you walk uphill for around ninety minutes. The map from the Pilgrim Office showed the hills, but I didn't expect it to be as steep as it was. It is literally all uphill. I know I wasn't the only pilgrim to be slightly apprehensive about what was to come. We'd all heard the Pyrenees were tough, but it was much worse.

After a pleasant-looking walk though farm fields, animals and rustic old buildings you come to a place called Orisson. Orisson has a beautiful albergue overlooking the start of the Pyrenees, and the view is absolutely stunning. It was now around 11am and a lot of pilgrims were deciding to stay in Orisson and continue the walk over the Pyrenees the next day. At first, I was undecided, because I didn't want to stop walking after just two hours, but I could feel how tired I was getting, so I decided to stay with the crowd and stop in Orisson for the night. The line to get a bed was pretty long, so I decided to get a beer from the bar and sit overlooking the magnificent view of the mountains, talking to fellow pilgrims about the deceiving hills we'd just climbed. The view from this albergue really is exquisite; I'd never seen anything like it.

When I finally got in line there were only a couple of people in front of me and I was soon asking for a bed, but I didn't get one. I asked the man behind the desk if there was a bed for me and he told me there was, so I paid the twenty-eight euros (very expensive if you ask me) and he asked for my pilgrim passport, so I reached into my bag and… it wasn't there! I searched, and I searched, and I searched. I had everything out of my bag, but it was just not there. All I can think of is that during the uphill walk I must have gotten my map out of my bag and not seen my pilgrim passport fall out, and without this you cannot stay in ANY albergues on the Camino. I searched every inch of my bag, knowing the pockets I was looking through would be empty.

I explain to the owner of the albergue what had happened, but he was having none of it. He told me I couldn't stay there without my passport, so I took a seat back outside and thought things through. I could keep walking, get into Spain, and hope that there was a Pilgrim Office where I could get another passport, or walk back to Saint-Jean, but both options were demoralising to me at that moment.

I made the decision to grab my bag and retrace my steps down the hills I'd just walked up, hoping I'd find my passport not so far away from the albergue. After more than an hour I gave up hope of finding it and realised the only option I had left was to walk back to Saint-Jean-Pied-de-Port. A devastating start to my Camino.

I can look back and laugh about it now, but at the time I could have cried, and at around 2pm on my first day of walking I arrived back in Saint-Jean, defeated and not very happy with the world. It wasn't the world's fault though; it was mine, and I was angry because usually I'm very careful and hardly lose anything. I went back to the Pilgrim Office and explained what had happened to the lady behind the counter, who in turn thought it was hilarious. I remember just giving her a blank stare while she was laughing, as I wasn't in a laughing mood. She gave me another passport and told me to get an albergue for the night, as it was too late to start walking again now. I could have walked back to Orisson, but I was defeated, and the beds would have been gone by now. I just wanted to forget about today and start afresh in the morning, so I did.

I found a lovely albergue that I'd missed the night before. It was called the Beilari and was run by a Spanish (I think) family who couldn't do enough for you. It was pricy at thirty euros but well worth it. The rooms were private(ish) and had three beds in each, so even though I was sharing with two other pilgrims it would be better than the night before. I just prayed no one would be snoring tonight. The price included a communal dinner with the other pilgrims and breakfast in the morning. It was a large, spacious old building, with Camino photos plastered over every wall. The communal dinner was in the back garden on large tables, holding all the pilgrims. I think there were twenty-one of us, if I remember correctly.

Before dinner the owner explained that he wanted us to all get to know each other and become friends, so he played 'breaking the ice' games with us as a group and it worked well. People started to talk and become friends. A lovely idea to make people interact with each other, and without this, I wouldn't have made two amazing friends I have today. We would throw an invisible ball to someone random and they would say their name, where they came from and why they were on the Camino. The invisible ball part looked ridiculous, people putting their arms out to catch a ball that wasn't there, but it worked.

There was a small Canadian woman sitting opposite me with frizzy, long grey hair (sorry Michele) but a great, friendly smile. First impressions have a big impact on how I am with people and Michele was the first person on the Camino I could tell had a lovely personality and a big heart. She has a little glint in her, Michele, and I can guarantee she was a bit of a fox back in the day. You can just tell with some people straightaway that they have a lovely soul, and she was one of those people. Little did I know at this time she would become a very important part of my Camino. Michele had the invisible ball and explained she was from Canada and doing the Camino for 'the experience of a lifetime'. She stopped talking and met my line of sight and threw me the imaginary ball. I'm quite loud and outspoken when I want to be, but in large groups I don't like talking. No one does, I imagine. I hadn't thought about what I was going to say and just sat there for a moment, stuck for words.

The owner of the albergue said to me, 'Just say your name, where you're from and why you're here. It's OK if you don't want to, though.'

I couldn't be the only one not to do it, so I began speaking, and said, 'I'm Jordan, I'm from Wales, and the only reason I'm here is because I lost my pilgrim passport on the way to Orisson and had to walk back down the mountain a couple of hours ago.'

With that everyone around the table started laughing and gave me a round of applause, the ice well and truly broken. I even managed to laugh at the situation myself, but only for a split second.

A very tall man with glasses came outside and apologised for being late, took his seat at the table and said hello to everybody. Looking at him I had the same feeling I had with Michele, that he was a nice person. But as I met his line of sight and smiled at him, he looked at the floor and didn't smile back. I get that a lot when I'm abroad and I think it's because I have tattoos, a shaved head and look like a bit of a thug. But when people get to know me, they soon realise that a thug is very, very far from who I am. I find it quite strange that people are put off by my tattoos as they're of a religious nature, but they tend to make people a bit wary of me. So anyway, I threw this invisible ball at the tall guy with glasses, and he explained that his name was Marc, he was from the Netherlands and he was walking the Camino to 'find himself on a great adventure'. I also didn't know at that moment that Marc was to become one of my best friends and someone to have a huge influence, not only on my Camino, but also on my life. To this day he is one of my closest friends in life and we talk four or five times a week over video call.

Once the games and dinner were finished, I decided to take a shower and relax. I went into the dining room, where they had a large wooden table, and sat next to a man I hadn't really noticed during the invisible ball session. He was looking at his map and explained to me that he was doing the Camino by bicycle, and that he'd never done anything like this before. He told me that his whole life had been planned, and since he was young, he'd known everything he was doing months in advance. He was extremely disciplined but woke up one morning and decided to do the Camino, and for the first time in his life he felt 'free'. His name was Fritz and like Marc, he was from the Netherlands, where he owned a café.

After around an hour Marc asked if he could sit with us and we all had a nice chat with a few beers. Marc and Fritz would unconsciously start talking Dutch and then apologise to me for being rude, but I didn't take it that way at all, and actually didn't mind. I like hearing other languages, even if I haven't got a clue what they're talking about. The three of us spoke about all the different things we were looking forward to seeing on the Camino, and it was nice to see other people getting excited about the same things as me.

In most albergues the doors lock, and the lights go off by 10-10:30. It seems early, but people start walking at 5am and need sleep, so it's reasonable. The owner of the albergue told us we needed to go upstairs to our beds, as we were the last ones and the albergue was locking up. Marc and Fritz went up before me as I'd just opened a beer and you couldn't take them upstairs, so I promised the owner I'd be in bed within ten minutes, and he agreed to let me stay downstairs. . I hadn't met the other two people in my room yet and prayed they were asleep and didn't snore, but as I crept through the door so as not to wake my roommates, I saw Marc and Fritz getting into bed. Brilliant! The Camino has a funny way of doing things like that. We all stayed up for another hour talking and having a laugh, before calling it a night and getting our heads down.

Marc and I knew we wouldn't see Fritz again as he was cycling the Camino and he'd do two to three of our days in just one day on his bike. You could easily do 40-50 miles (64-80km) a day on a bike, while 20 miles (32km) a day walking is classed as a very, very good day, so we shook his hand and said our goodbyes before going to sleep. Then, after about thirty minutes, it started again, the dreaded snoring. I was in a deep sleep, and when I've had a drink, it's nearly impossible to wake me. . My parents have full on shaken me and screamed at me (normally when I fall asleep drunk on the bathroom floor) and I still haven't woken up. But the snoring coming from Fritz that night had no problem waking me. He sounded like a train blowing its horn. I even shook him and shout 'FRITZ!' really loud at one point, but he was out of it and I was wide awake. Marc also woke up at one point, but he had no problem getting back to sleep, leaving me very jealous. It was 2am when I finally got to sleep, by that time I was completely sober and had beaten my phone at Solitaire about twelve times.

Saint-Jean-Pied-de-Port – Roncesvalles 25.1km

Marc had his alarm set for 5am, so after three hours of sleep I was getting ready to tackle the hills once more and to head for the Pyrenees. Surprisingly, I felt really good and was looking forward to it and knew it couldn't get any worse than yesterday… but it did. Another lesson learned: don't speak to soon.

Fritz was still asleep, and Marc was having breakfast when I left. I'm not really a breakfast person and skip it regularly, so I was gone before them both. It was still relatively dark when I left the albergue but there were many pilgrims on the road, and some had even set off at around 4am. I started from where I'd started the day before and got on my way. This time I made sure I wouldn't lose anything. Tackling the hills was just as hard, but I completed them about thirty minutes quicker than I had the day before. I arrived back at the albergue in Orisson but decided I wasn't going to stop there today, and I would cross the whole Pyrenees in just one day. A few pilgrims who'd done the Camino previously warned me against this, telling me to stay in Orisson and split the Pyrenees into two days, but I decide to go on, determined to do it in one go and catch up on the day before. The whole thing took me over nine hours and was easily the single, most difficult thing I have ever done in my life and that is not an exaggeration.

The Pyrenees is one of the most dangerous mountain ranges in Europe, with steep climbs, unpredictable weather and sheer drops from cliffs. As I explained earlier, you must walk 1,400 metres above sea level to cross the border into Spain and it's all uphill. You very rarely see any flat paths on the mountains, and it's soul destroying when you conquer a massive hill up the side of a mountain, just to see another hill twice as bad as the one before – but somehow you just keep going. No matter how much your legs hurt or how tired you are, you keep going. Your body can do amazing things when pushed to its limits and the Pyrenees will prove that to you.

I must also point out that some people on the Camino say the Pyrenees are easy and don't know what all the fuss is about, but I shall tell you the difference. I was talking to one girl who walked the mountains a day before me and completed it in five and half hours. She told me that it was a nice walk and she barely struggled at all. That's because the day she walked it, the mountains were covered in light fog and it was 18 degrees at its hottest. It even rained for two hours of her walk. I would have had no problem with the Pyrenees in that weather, either. On the day I walked it, the coolest the weather got was 34 degrees and the hottest soared in at 40 degrees on top of the mountain. Walking up hill with 12kg on your back for nine hours, in 45-degree heat, can kill a person, that's a fact. So, if anyone tells you that the Pyrenees is a walk in the park, they are either lying, have done it in very cool weather or are a very experienced hiker. I won't take anything away from the Pyrenees though; it is beautiful. The views from some of the mountains are like a postcard, and you'll be in awe of its beauty.

I soon came to a statue of the Virgin Mary, known as the *Vierge d'Orisson*, a tranquil figure keeping watch over the magnificent mountain views. The shrine was draped with offerings from pilgrims, including pairs of boots, photographs of deceased love ones and letters of prayer, all left at the feet of Mary. It was here I met two Australian girls called Emma and Ally. They hadn't come on the Camino together but met up on the mountain, while I met them during a water stop. That's another thing I want to point out – take plenty of water with you up on the mountains. There aren't a lot of fountains to fill up from and the lack of water up there can be dangerous.

Emma and Alley were experienced hikers compared to me and I could tell they wanted to walk faster, as I was slowing them down, but I take my hat off to them. They kept at my pace and we all had a great laugh while walking the most dreaded hills I've ever seen. I live in the South Wales valleys and my town is surrounded by mountains, so I thought I would do OK, but none of them are this scale. After about five hours of walking through some of the most beautiful sights I've ever seen, I needed to rest. The heat was unbearable, and I knew I had such a long way to go yet. The sweat was absolutely dripping from me, and I was drenched from head to foot, so I found a tree with a big shadow and decided to get some shade.

I told Emma and Alley I would catch them up and laid down with my head on my backpack, wondering to myself, 'What the hell are you doing, Jordan? You should have just gone to Ibiza with your friends. Now you're stuck on this mountain and will probably die before you reach the bottom.' I didn't believe that, though, it was just me thinking the worst again. Plus, I'm not an Ibiza kind of person.

I must have dozed off, because the next thing I knew I was being shaken awake by a group of American girls who thought I'd fainted from the heat. I'd fallen asleep and rolled over. With my head not on my backpack anymore it looked like I'd fainted. I explained to the girls I was resting and had fallen asleep, so they laughed and continued walking.

Embarrassing, to say the least, but when you need to stop and rest, you listen to your body and do it.

I soon started walking again and caught up with the girls who'd just 'saved me'. I started walking with one of them who was at the back of their group. Her name was Tiffany (name changed) and she was from California. She had big, beautiful eyes, a stunning smile and a very artistic tattoo on her left arm. You know sometimes when you talk to someone and you don't mean to flirt, but it just happens? We had that straightaway, and it was clear we both fancied each other. Neither of us said anything, though, and we continued to chat and flirt for around an hour, when I found myself needing another rest.

When I get hungry, my body will feel weak instantly, and I will start to shake. It's something to do with my sugar, according to my doctor, but isn't serious. It's just my body telling me to eat, but for this to start happening on the Pyrenees mountains was terrible for me. I knew my already slow pace would now become snail-like and I would feel like crap the whole way to the end. I told Tiffany to walk on without me while I had another rest and tried to compose myself, but again I fell asleep. This time I woke up on my own after being asleep for about twenty minutes. I felt a bit better now and straight in front of me I saw an apple tree I hadn't seen previously. I tipped the only water I had left over the apples to wash them and ate four, then, after another ten-minute rest, my legs started to calm down from the shaking, but not completely. I decided now was going to be the time I needed to push forward, because if the hunger and shaking started again I'd be in trouble. It was close to 40 degrees on these mountains, so I needed to move as fast as I could and get to Roncesvalles, and I did just that. I covered around four miles in the next hour, and even though that doesn't seem a lot, it is a considerable amount in that heat and going uphill.

I realised I was now at a pinnacle point on the mountains as I was greeted by a cattle grid and stone border marking, telling me I was now in Spain. I placed one foot to the left of the marker and one to the right, making me in two countries at exactly the same time – the right side of my body in Spain, the left side of my body in France. I've always wanted to do that. I took some photos and was quickly on my way.

I looked at my guidebook and saw I wasn't far (4km) from the highest point of the mountains, the Col de Lepoeder. It was a gentler climb through woodland for the next stage and I soon found myself at the peak, a high of 1,450 metres above sea level. At the top I was surprised to see a big wooden information board and an emergency telephone, for troubled pilgrims. It's worth pointing out that all the way up the Pyrenees you will see numbers spray-painted onto trees. If you're ever in trouble and must phone the emergency services, give them the number you last saw, as it will help them locate you a lot quicker. Many people who've broken ankles, fallen down cliffs or had heat exhaustion have used these markings to save their own lives.

At the peak of the mountains I had a choice. I could either take the less steep route down the mountain, but this would take me considerably longer, or take the extremely steep, but quicker, route through the largest remaining beech forest in Europe. I decided on the quicker route to get to Roncesvalles faster – probably the wrong choice. It's 6km downhill and is a 79 percent decline. Very steep indeed!! But it's covered by trees both sides and I guess it's still better than walking uphill in the sun. These woods were absolutely beautiful, though, but just as I was enjoying the walk downhill my legs started to shake again; I could hardly gather the strength to keep my legs stiff as I walked.

'This is all I need,' I said to myself. The remaining distance seemed to last forever, and what should have taken me around an hour took me near enough two and a half. I had to rest and find fruit on several occasions. A handful of berries would do; I would have taken anything, and I did. I thought that even if I got sick, I could rest a few days and recover, I just needed to eat anything I could get my hands on to get me off this mountain (shouldn't have skipped breakfast).

On reaching the bottom of the hill I saw an amazing sight in the shape of a river and I didn't waste any time in stripping off and jumping straight in, as shallow as it was. (I had underpants on, don't worry). I just lay there, cooling off, and wondering to myself how I ever managed to complete those mountains. I was physically broken but was so proud of myself and, looking back, I realise how lucky I was to get down from there.

I got dressed and had been sitting by the side of the river for around twenty minutes when I saw a load of pilgrims walk past me in 'normal' clothes. I recognised them from Saint-Jean and asked them how far it was to Roncesvalles. One of the guys in the group said to me, 'I did the same thing – thought I was miles away and stopped by the river for a break. It's actually there,' and he pointed through some trees where the path continued.

I walked about ten steps through the trees, looked right and saw hundreds of pilgrims waiting in line in front of a massive albergue. I didn't care about the hordes of pilgrims waiting before me, all I wanted was food and sleep. I was a very happy boy at this stage and got in line.

Even though the Pyrenees are tough, this experience of it was my own. You might find it a walk in the park and think I'm a drama queen, but for me it was extremely difficult. It was also the most beautiful mountain range I'd seen so far in my life. The statue of the Virgin Mary and the crossing into Spain were particular highlights, but the scenery is out of this world.

I got in line, and during my wait for a bed I saw Michele from Saint-Jean, the Canadian woman who threw the invisible ball at me. She told me she'd seen Marc in Orisson, and he'd given her a message for me: 'I'm staying in Orisson tonight, so I'll catch up with you in a few days.'

I was quite gutted. I was looking forward to seeing Marc tonight and swapping stories of the Pyrenees, but he hadn't even started it yet, so I thanked Michele and stayed waiting in line. There were about six people in front of me when the guy behind the counter shouted out, 'Sorry everyone, all beds are now taken. No more room at the inn.'

You must excuse my French, but I said out loud to myself, 'You have to be fucking kidding me.' That was the last thing I wanted to hear after today. Surely, he could see the line in front of him and knew there weren't enough beds long before he told us. Some parts of the albergue were under maintenance and not all the beds were available, making spaces limited.

It turned out to be a good thing in the end, as at the top of town there was a hotel called La Posada. I enjoyed a private room, own toilet and shower and double bed, all for just fifty euros. It was just what I needed after that day, so I checked in. I took my bag upstairs, threw it on the bed, locked the door and walked back downstairs for some food. I had to eat quickly, and the chef was kind enough to sort me out a huge piece of steak. It didn't take me long to get through it, washing it down with a very large glass of beer.

By the time I'd waited in line, not got a bed, checked into the other hotel and had food, it was around 20:30. I'd planned on taking a shower after the hot day and the amount of walking I'd done, but as I got to the room I literally belly-flopped onto the bed. I woke up at 8:30 the next morning, no snoring in the world would have woken me up that night.

Looking back on the Pyrenees now I really don't know how I did it. With a mixture of no sleep for the previous two nights due to people snoring, 40-degree heat, no food, no water and feeling like absolute shit, I really don't know how I managed to finish it. Like I said before, the human body can do amazing things when you need it to. Don't let what I've said put you off – get yourself up and over that mountain. In the months and years after the Camino, you will be glad you did it and will want to do it all over again. Walking over the Pyrenees mountains is one of my biggest accomplishments to date, along with completing the whole Camino. Things I'm immensely proud of and talk about any chance I get.

Waking up at 8:30 was not what I'd planned. I'd wanted to start walking at 5am to miss more astonishing heat, but I was so tired I forgot to put my alarm on. When I finally crawled out of bed, I felt a very nasty blister on the bottom of my left foot and decided I ain't walking anywhere today. I had as much time as I needed to complete the Camino; rushing it and walking in pain was not something that appealed to me. Plus, I could hold back a day and meet up with Marc and hopefully walk together to Pamplona over the days to follow.

I was showered, dressed and packed by 9:30, and out of the hotel and sitting in the bar downstairs. I had breakfast, a cup of hot chocolate and a wait for the albergue to open. Today I would be the first one there and there would be no chance of me missing out on a bed. I hung around for a bit by the river, took another little snooze under the sun and got into the albergue at around 11am.

I went in, got my passport stamped, paid the eight euros for a bed and they told me I was in bed number two. I wondered to myself who could have gotten there so quickly as to get bed number one.

As I was putting my passport back into my bag, I could see this figure standing in front me, but I ignored it for a while, thinking it was one of the albergue workers. After a few seconds the figure began moving closer and closer towards me, so I looked up and it was Marc, with a big cheesy grin on his face. He'd got bed number one, so we had a small chat and took our bags upstairs.

Marc explained to me that he'd set off from Orisson at 5am and had done the Pyrenees in just under six hours. He told me it was cloudy up on the mountains and he'd even had a bit of rain, so it was nice and cool.

'Alright for some' I thought. I told him my experience with the heat and the hunger, and he told me I should have stayed in Orisson with him and done the Pyrenees over two days. He didn't need to tell me that, I already knew.

I went back down to the river while Marc got showered and changed. We'd agreed to go for a beer, and he would meet me outside when he was ready.

After around forty minutes I decided to walk to the bar, thinking Marc would know where I was and would meet me there. As I stood up to begin walking, I heard the bell of a bicycle behind me. 'Ring, ring, ring, ring, ring.' I remembered thinking that someone was eager for me to move out of the way. I looked back and was happy to see that it was Fritz.

Fritz was the last person I expected to see as he should have been a good 100km in front of me. But nope, here he was, riding up behind me with a big smile on his face.

'Jordan, I am here,' he shouted in his thick Dutch accent.

'Bloody hell, Fritz, you got lost, did you?' I replied as a joke.

'That's exactly what happened, my friend,' he replied, laughing hysterically.

I told him to quickly go and get a bed and to meet us in the bar just up the street as soon as he was ready.

Marc finally arrived at the bar and while he was having a cup of tea, I started to tell him about Fritz. He didn't believe me, as Fritz should have been way in front.

'It was someone who looked like him,' Marc kept saying.

'I spoke to him. It was Fritz, trust me,' I kept replying.

Marc can be stubborn when he thinks he's right, but about fifteen minutes later Fritz walked in, beaming from ear to ear, and Marc couldn't believe it. They hugged and shook hands, then Fritz and I did the same.

We asked how he was in Roncesvalles when he should be so far in front. Turns out Fritz took a wrong turn on the mountains and got very lost. He then tired himself out getting back to the right path. He was a day behind everyone else who started on a bike the same time as him, but Marc and I were happy about it, as we had another night of drinking with our new friend Fritz.

Fritz admitted that, fitness-wise, he'd underestimated the Pyrenees and it was much harder than he thought, and so did I. Even though I believe he did get lost, I believe fitness played a bigger part and he was tired. But it's not easy on a bike, so all credit to him for beating those mountains.

We sat drinking and laughing for most of the afternoon and into the night. We talked and laughed about anything and everything and really got to know each other that night. Marc and Fritz are wonderful, interesting people who I could happily talk to for hours and never get bored. Marc doesn't really give a lot away about himself and is private, a lot like me. But Fritz, even though he looks mean and scary from the outside, is a big softie and is quite an emotional guy and cries when the subject turns to parents. He loved his father dearly and witnessed his death. Even though it was a long time ago it still upsets Fritz, and it was strange to see a man you hardly know cry to you about such personal things. But the Camino brings that out in people, it really does.

Marc kept quiet but did say how much he missed his mother and how much he would love to see her again. There is a big sadness in Marc that I've seen all along the Camino and still see now, five years later. I don't think he's ever gotten over his mother's death and it eats away at him, which is very sad, as he's an amazing man. I learned another lesson that night: Don't take your parents for granted. You get one mother and one father, look after them.

My biggest nightmare is my parents dying and even though I know it will come one day, I don't think you can ever be prepared for something like that. I went outside the bar to phone my parents and my nan to tell them I was OK, that I loved them, and I would speak to them in a couple of days. One day I won't be able to do that, so I'd make the most of it while I could, and I still do now. I must point out that when I say Marc and I had a beer, it was actually just me having a beer, because Marc doesn't drink, at all. Marc and I are so different in life you wouldn't have thought he and I would even speak, never mind be such good friends as we are today, but opposites attract, I suppose.

By 9pm Fritz and I were blind drunk and laughing at everything, but we had a superb evening, one of my favourite Camino nights. In all honesty, I can't remember walking back to the albergue from the bar and getting into bed. But I woke up in bed at 5am when Marc's alarm went off. If either Marc or Fritz put me there, I don't know, but thank you if either of you did.

When Marc and I woke up, Fritz was nowhere to be seen, as he was in bed number forty-something, so he wasn't close to us. Turned out he'd left early to try and make up some time he'd lost. Last night would turn out to be the last time we would see Fritz, but Marc and I kept in contact with him by email and he and Marc have since met up back in Holland a few times.

Don't count on much in Roncesvalles as there are no shops, banks or anything useful in sight, as it's very small.

Roncesvalles translates to 'Valley of Thorns' and only has a population of around seventy people. It's famous for the defeat of Charlemagne and the death of Roland in 778. Thousands of people every year start their pilgrimage to Santiago in Roncesvalles, missing out the Pyrenees Mountains. But come on, where is the fun in that?

Roncesvalles – Zubiri
22km

So today we were walking from Roncesvalles to Zubiri. As you leave Roncesvalles, you're instantly greeted by the famous 'SANTIAGO DE COMPOSTELA 790' (km) sign, with a lot of woodland directly behind it. It's one of the most famous signs and photographs of the Camino. You're bound to have seen it while doing your Camino research.

These woods come with a bit of history, as in Navarra during the 1700s local witches would meet in these woods and sacrifice children. By 1794 so many children had gone missing or had been found dead, they put up a 10-foot white cross to try and scare the witches away. Underneath the white cross there is a plaque with all the details. Even without reading the plague you get a strange feeling in these woods, a very spooky place. As you pass through, you veer right onto a dirt path and after around 2.5km you enter a little village called Burguete. Hotel Burguete was a common stomping ground of Ernest Hemingway, and in its lobby, you can find an old piano bearing his signature that he dated 25/07/1923. You don't really see any towns from now on until you hit Zubiri. The towns you do pass through are very small and I didn't stop to look around.

The walk that day was either flat or downhill and was quite easy, passing next to farms or through woodland. Marc and I walked and talked for a while until he picked up pace and went on in front. I knew he was stopping in Zubiri, though, so I would see him later. I took pictures of cows, donkeys, pigs, the beautiful trees and a few selfies with some chickens, as I really enjoyed the walk. If only the rest of the Camino was this easy, but that wouldn't be fun now, would it?

After a good 14-mile (23km) walk, I reached the town of Zubiri. While I was passing through some woods there was a teenager sitting on a rock handing out leaflets for an albergue, I didn't like this too much as I felt it was just commercialising the Camino even more, and it took away the suspense of waiting to find out what your albergue is going to be like. Ends up he was advertising the albergue I ended up staying in. This was called Suseia, a new albergue that had only been open a few weeks. It was an exceptionally nice place with a communal living room, television and vending machines. It was here I started to speak to a Spanish girl. I can't remember her name, but she was with her parents and younger sister. Her father and I bumped into each other a lot on the Pyrenees mountains, and even though we couldn't speak a word to each other, we would say *'Amigo'* and high five every time we crossed paths. It was funny and he would laugh hysterically every time. Turned out they also took a rest day after the Pyrenees and were again walking on the same day as me. His daughter spoke perfect English and was very good company that night in Zubiri, a very funny girl. The first time I saw her she RAN, yes RAN past me on the Pyrenees. She was a running enthusiast back home in Barcelona and belonged to running and gymnastics groups and was by far the fittest person I saw on the Camino. She ran parts of the Pyrenees and hardly broke a sweat. From Roncesvalles to Zubiri she'd also been running, her family walking around two hours behind her each day. She asked me to guess her age and I honestly thought she was about twenty-two, but when she told me she was fifteen I was even more impressed, if not slightly embarrassed that a fifteen-year-old kid ran past me on a mountain while I was gasping for air and couldn't walk any further. It's funny now and we both laughed about it in Zubiri.

The thing is, though, I'm quite fit and haven't got a problem walking and running usually. OK, the cigarettes don't help, but I'm reasonably fit. The lack of food, water and sleep were my downfall that day, my own entire fault.

At around 6pm she joined Marc and me in having dinner, but I still didn't catch her name. It's a shame, as I would have liked to have kept it touch to see how she got on in life, as I'm convinced she's going to be a famous athlete or gymnastics star one day.

I had tomato pasta that night, sprinkled with cheese, and a large orange juice. I was finally starting to feel like I was on the Camino. The change in food and meeting so many wonderful, different people was doing me the world of good, and I couldn't wait to start walking again in the morning.

After dinner, the Spanish Superwoman returned to her family and Marc and I went to the river in Zubiri for a look. There were a lot of pilgrims swimming in the river, a lot of them female and topless, so Marc decided to go inside the bar for a coffee. I, on the other hand, decided to stay outside and enjoy the view. Marc is married with children and I must say, he is so devoted to his family that he wouldn't even look at these women, and I really admired that about that him. He loves them with all his heart and told me: 'I don't need to look at those women, Jordan, I have a wife I love dearly and that's enough for me.'

I live in a small South Wales town called Mountain Ash, an old coal mining community in the valleys, and even though a lot of people live here, it's not very big at all. According to the internet, in 2001, 7,000 people lived here. I think that's probably up to the 10,000 mark by now. Even though 10,000 doesn't seem a lot, it is more than the average population of other small towns in Wales. Nothing very exciting happens in Mountain Ash, but it does have a famous race every New Year's Eve called the Nos Galan, where people come from all over the world to take part in running through the streets. Every year they have a mystery runner who is a famous athlete, and this has attracted some big names in the past, with Linford Christie being one. I've run three times in the past, and one year, in the under-fourteen's category, I came ninth out of eighty-seven kids. But the next year I came last because I didn't look where I was going and ran into a parked car. As you've heard, Mountain Ash is small. So, what would the chances be that I would run into someone from Mountain Ash on the Camino? Well it happened… Kind of.

I was sitting in a bar with Marc in Zubiri hiding from the boobs, when a guy overheard a conversation we were having and heard my thick, Welsh accent.

'What part of Wales are you from, my friend?' he asks.

I tell him I'm from Mountain Ash and his face drops.

'I was born in Mountain Ash hospital,' he says in excitement.

I couldn't believe it. Part of why I travel so much is to get away from the place and the people, so I really didn't expect to see someone from home in a tiny town in Spain, doing the same walk as me. Turns out he left Mountain Ash when he was fourteen and had lived in Cardiff and England since, so we didn't know the same people or anything, but a small world, none the less.

Marc got to Zubiri before me that day and his albergue was at the start of town, while mine was about a five-minute walk to the other side. We said our good nights and I turned in at around 20:30, while Marc did the same. I talked to the Spanish father, my '*amigo*', for a bit, while his daughter translated for us both. He's a funny guy and it's a shame I didn't see them again after that night, but I hope they all had a very good Camino.

I got to sleep at around 10pm and thankfully the other nine people in my room didn't snore.

Zubiri means 'Bridge Village' in Basque and the town dates to around the year 900. It has a population of around 450 and has such facilities as a grocery shop, bank and a church.

I had a cracking night's sleep, and was awake 5am, ready for the new day.

Zubiri – Pamplona
24km

Zubiri to Pamplona is around 24km and there are a few cafés on the way. I decided to stop at nearly all of them. I wasn't in a rush today and the walking was easy.

I soon came to a town called Trinidad de Arre which has shops, restaurants and a pilgrim hospital that has existed since the eleventh century. You pass many towns on this day that can offer a bed or something to eat; The walk is very peaceful and once more surrounded by farm fields. But as you come into Pamplona you walk next to a main road leading into the city. There was a massive error on my part, as I'd totally forgotten about the San Fermín (running of the bulls) festival that was happening in Pamplona at this time. Walking through the streets was chaos and I literally couldn't move. I've never seen so many people packed into little, narrow streets like this before. Passing through the main square, which should have taken me ten minutes, now took forty minutes as I tried to push through the crowds.

It was here in Pamplona that I would be leaving Marc for a while. He'd booked his bed months in advance, in a private hostel near the city centre. He told me this on the morning of walking into Pamplona, so I went around as many hotels, hostels and albergues as I possibly could, but the cheapest room I could find was nearly 400 euros (372 euros in fact). I decided I couldn't look around forever and that the only thing I could do was keep walking past Pamplona, something I really didn't want to do.

The next place I could walk to that had an albergue was Cizur Menor, another 5km away, so I decided to get walking. I'd wanted to see the bulls running through Pamplona for years, but totally forgot that it was this time of year and was sad to be missing it.

The walk was horrible and was next to roads the whole 5km out of town and I was really gutted to be leaving Pamplona. I covered the distance in just over an hour and found an albergue. On getting a bed and settling in, I heard a welcoming voice say, 'Well hello, Welshman.'

It was the lovely Michele. I actually thought she was behind me at this point, but she was here and greeted me with a hug. Michele is such a nice woman and it always brightened up my day when I bumped into her. We caught up in the albergue's garden and chilled out for the rest of the day.

When I arrived I had two very big blisters on my left foot and was in a lot of discomfort, until the owner of the albergue showed me something that would make my Camino a whole lot easier, so I'll share it with you and hope it helps. She was a small, elderly lady who spoke good English. She told me she'd worked and lived in England, while she was training to be a nurse in the 1960s. After she'd stamped my passport and told me the house rules, I stood up, and she noticed me limping slightly. Before I knew it, she was hurrying me into her living room and ordering me to take my boots and socks off.

'I'll take care of your blisters,' she told me.

I wasn't going to say no, she was an ex-nurse and would know her stuff. She got a little syringe out of a first aid box and started to drain my blisters. It was a bit strange at first, a woman I didn't know draining my blisters for me in her living room while her husband sat there smiling at me, nodding his head in an agreeable manner. After the draining was done, she put on some disinfectant and bandaged up my feet. I was very grateful, and the pain was much better to cope with.

'I'll show you a trick,' she said. 'I'll be right back.'

I waited for around two or three minutes in her living room, while her elderly husband was still staring at me, smiling.

The lady walked back into the room and held up two sanitary towels.

I honestly didn't know what the hell was going to happen and started to feel quite uneasy. She then ripped out the insoles of my walking boots and stuck the sanitary towels to them, one on each insole.

'Put your boots back on,' she said.

I did what I was told and walked up and down her living room, trying out my new insoles, and seriously, people, it was like heaven! It was like walking on a cloud. I couldn't feel any pain and the walking was so soft it put a massive smile on my face, as I'd been limping all day in some pain.

She then ordered me to 'Buy some sanitary towels from the supermarket and change them every three days. If you do that, you won't get another blister all Camino.'

And I'm very happy to say I followed her instructions, and she was right, not one more blister for the whole walk. Try it guys, it works!

The sanitary towel absorbs the moisture that helps start a blister and it cushions your step. It was a marvellous thing for her to do for me and I will always be thankful. A Camino without blisters was a godsend for me.

Also, that night I had a shoulder massage from an elderly Australian woman who I'd noticed had been staring at me quite a bit. It was funny, she was sleeping on the top bunk above Michele, and I'd asked Michele if she was any good at shoulder massages, as I had a lot of pain from carrying my bag. I hadn't even finished my sentence and the old Australian woman leapt out of bed, pulled me onto a chair, pulled my shirt over my head and started rubbing my shoulders. Michele and I looked at each other in a bit of shock, but it was so funny that we still laugh about it now. That was a good day for me afterwards, with my blisters getting sorted and a shoulder massage. How lucky was I, eh? You soon learn to say yes to the kindness people offer you on the Camino.

Michele and I were then sitting in the garden with a glass of wine when at 8pm I had a message on social media. It was from Marc.

'I am staying in Pamplona one more night, come back tomorrow. I have found you a bed for fifty euros.'

I was ecstatic and I went to bed with a huge smile on my face, knowing I could finally see the bulls run through the famous streets of Pamplona.

Cizur Menor is famous in Spain for its meat, and even though it's only a small place, people from miles around travel here to taste the rich flavours. On entering the village, you'll see the Church of San Miguel, which was once part of a monastery for pilgrims. It was left derelict in the mid-1800s but was saved from ruin by the government of Navarra. You have bus stops, a cash machine, a supermarket and a pharmacy here, so if you forget to top up on essentials in Pamplona, here is your place.

The next morning, I was up at 5:30 and I caught the 7:03 bus back to Pamplona to meet Marc. (I'd walked it once; I wasn't walking it again.) He met me at the bus station in the centre of the city and took me to the hostel he was staying at, around a ten-minute walk. The hostel felt a lot different from an albergue, even though the rooms were the same. The difference was the people; there are no pilgrims in hostels, and it seemed strange having to explain to the people in the hostel what the Camino de Santiago is. Marc and I didn't like it; we wanted to be surrounded by pilgrims, but the main reason I came back here was to watch the running of the bulls.

Marc and I walked down to the main street and he found it absolutely hilarious that at 8:30 in the morning I went to have a burger and fries in a fast-food restaurant. I knew it was early, but I hadn't eaten properly for around fifteen hours, and it was the only place open, so I had to eat. He sat there and laughed and laughed, because apparently that isn't heard of in Holland. Good job he doesn't live in the UK.

We watched the people climbing onto wooden gates, statues, climbing onto anything they could find, just to get a better view of the bulls. Marc and I got into a good spot on the main street, hidden in a doorway that the bulls would run past, but we were quickly moved on by the police. Only the runners and the bulls are allowed on the main street. We walked up to the top of town, dressed in our white San Fermín shirts and red Pamplona scarves, which we'd both just bought. We really looked the part, just like the thousands of people with us. We found a good spot on the edge of the arena that the bulls and runners would enter after racing through the streets. We watched a man of about twenty-five years old get knocked flying by one of these beasts, who landed face first and needed urgent medical treatment. All the bulls ran past us with vicious force and into the arena.

We decided to go into the arena and watch the bullfighting afterwards, witnessing men getting thrown up in the air while the crowds went wild. What we didn't realise is during this arena stage, the bulls are stabbed and poked to make them angry before someone slits their throats in front of the whole arena. I'm sorry, but I'm not OK with that. Marc and I got up and left. Such pointless, harrowing deaths of beautiful animals is not something I wished to witness. But I suppose that's part of travelling. Sometimes you'll see things you don't like, but it's all part of the experience.

After the experience with the bulls we decided to explore Pamplona some more. I can imagine it's a totally different city when the bulls are not running. Little cafés and bakeries everywhere, it's a lovely place, and some time I will visit again to explore on a larger scale.

After a while walking around and pushing through the many people in the streets, Marc suggested we go for some food. He told me he fancied some steak and being a steak-lover myself, I was all for it. It didn't turn out great, though, and I still wind him up to this day over what happened.

Because of the festival in Pamplona, the streets and parks were filled with food tents serving different kinds of meats. We walked around for a while and chose a tent that had tables and chairs for us to sit. The steak they were cooking looked amazing and Marc decided that this was the place for us. I was happy to go along with whatever he wanted. One of my friends back home phoned me at this point, and as Marc was asking the prices of the meat, I stepped aside to speak on the phone. When I ended the call, Marc was already seated drinking lemonade, and I asked the tent owner for the same.

The tent was huge and had a big coal pit where I noticed there was A LOT of meat cooking but thought nothing of it. A few minutes later a waiter brought out a huge plate of four steaks and a pile of fries. Marc and I agreed on two steaks each and I ate most of the fries. Halfway through my second steak the waiter brought out two massive plates of mushrooms and an equal amount of vegetables, before coming back out with even more steak and even more fries. I asked Marc what was going on and he told me he'd ordered them.

'It's only twelve euros,' he said.

Marc can speak very good English but between him and the little English-speaking tent owner, some wires got crossed. We'd been served seven plates by this point.

'Marc, there's no way on this earth all this costs twelve euros,' I said sternly.

I think to begin with, he thought it was an all-you-can-eat for twelve euros, but I could see in his eyes that by this point he was starting to doubt himself.

He called the waiter over, pointed at the steak and asked, 'How much?'

The waiter responded, 'Twelve euros, sir'

'See, I told you, twelve euros, it's a bargain,' Marc said, with a grin on his face.

I still couldn't see how this much food could cost twelve euros though, so, I said to the waiter, 'Is it twelve euros total or twelve euros per plate?'

'It is twelve euros per plate, sir,' was the devastating reply.

I looked at Marc and could see the smirk he was wearing fall from his face. His eyes widened and his jaw hit the floor. The look on his face still makes me laugh. At this moment in time I'm sitting at home writing this, thinking about the look of dread that overcame him, and I'm laughing my head off.

'So how much is the total so far?' I asked.

'With drinks, sir, ninety euros,' and he handed us the bill.

Now Marc is a man of few words and doesn't like to cause a fuss or say anything that people might not like. During the whole Camino, if something needed to be said, it was me who would say it, as I'm the one that doesn't give a shit (Marc's words not mine). But on this occasion, Marc came into his own and really wasn't happy. He got quite angry and flustered, so far away from what he is usually like.

'The owner told me it was all twelve euros, why did he say that if it wasn't true??'

He wasn't holding back and even though he wasn't shouting, he was talking loud enough for me to put my head in my hands and hide from the world. It went quiet for a second, but as I looked up, he started again.

'Ninety euros for two people is too much. You're robbing us, and we're not paying for it'.

So far, we'd had three plates of steak (thirty-six euros), two plates of fries (twenty-four euros), a plate of mushrooms (twelve euros) and a plate of vegetables (twelve euros), plus drinks. The owner of the food tent came out and asked us what the problem was, which enticed Marc to go off on one again.

'The problem is, is that you said it was twelve euros and it isn't. It's twelve euros per plate, and we're not paying ninety euros,' he told him. 'Have these plates and take them back, we don't want them,' he shouted.

The tent owner went on to say that since the meat had been eaten and as Marc ordered it, we must pay, and to be honest, I agreed. I honestly believe it was just miscommunication and they didn't understand each other, not that the tent owner was a liar. But it was ordered, and it was our fault for not double-checking the prices, so I agreed to pay. Marc didn't, though, and things were getting a bit heated now between him and the tent owner, so I decided to step in. I told the tent owner we would give him fifty euros and leave, because it was partly his fault for not explaining the prices properly. I told him in future, he should put up a sign and explain that it's twelve euros per plate, as to foreigners it's confusing.

Like I said, though, it was more our fault, so I didn't mind paying if we had to, but thankfully, he agreed to my cut down offer of fifty euros. Marc and I paid twenty-five euros each and were on our way. Marc couldn't apologise enough to me and I told him repeatedly it was OK. He's still angry, though. I never let him forget it and teased him about it the whole Camino…

I still do now.

On walking around the town, we saw two Buddhist monks greeting people and handing out little pieces of paper, and Marc and I were given a piece each. One of the Buddhists was sitting on a chair, while the other one sat on his friend's head! You know you're seeing street magic that makes them look like they're floating, but you know there's a long pole hidden somewhere holding them up – that kind of thing. The writing on the paper was meant to signify something about you or your life. Marc's had, 'Peace comes from within, do not seek it without.' Marc took this as a sign, because part of being on the Camino for him was wanting to make peace with himself. He had a few self-loathing issues that he wanted to get over on the Camino. I don't see why, because he's a lovely bloke, he just doesn't see it himself and that is sad. My paper said, 'Life is a dream, realise it.' I wouldn't make any connection to this until I arrived in Santiago but kept the paper safe inside the pages of my passport (still there to this day).

Marc and I decided to head back to the hostel, a nice little place with a lovely living room area. Hard to find, though, as there's no sign outside and it looks like a rundown, disused building. We sat and talked in the living room for a while with a beer (Marc was drinking coffee) and played a game of chess. Marc beat me.

We were both relieved to be walking again tomorrow, as neither of us liked playing the tourist today and missed the feeling of the Camino. Seeing the pilgrims, getting up early and getting to the next place after five or six hours of walking are all things us pilgrims look forward to, and it didn't feel right being a tourist for the day, so after a while we called it a day and headed to our beds. We had an early night at around 19:45 and I slept well, so I was raring to go in the morning.

Pamplona is so rich in history that you'll have to do your own research if you want in-depth information. I know bits, but nothing compared to how much this great city has been through over the years. What I do know is the city has a population of around 350,000 and was made world-famous in 1926 by the Ernest Hemingway novel, *The Sun Also Rises*. The book is about a group of American and British expatriates who travel from France to the San Fermín festival, to watch the running of the bulls and the bullfights. If you haven't read the book, you need to. In 75 BC the area was a campsite for the Roman general Pompey. He's the one thought to have called the area Pompaelo (which changed to Pamplona over the years that followed). In 2003 a Muslim cemetery was unearthed below the Castle Square, and over 200 human remains were found, giving us some indication that there was an important Muslim presence here at some point in Pamplona's history. Pamplona is listed as having one of the highest standards of living and quality of life in Spain. Statistics show crime is very low compared to the rest of Spain, but housing is expensive. Here you will find an airport, train station, bus station, many banks, restaurants and shops. This is a proper city and I recommend taking a rest day here and exploring.

Pamplona – Puente La Reina 25km

The next day's walk was Pamplona to Puente La Reina, a 25km walk that took us just under five hours. Our fitness was starting to improve, and we noticed we were starting to walk a lot quicker. As I left the city, I found myself walking next to the busy roads I'd completed two days earlier. This time, though, I didn't mind. I'd been to the San Fermín festival and I was now happy.

After an hour or so, I walked back through Cizur Menor and past the albergue I'd slept at. This time, though, I didn't stop and walked straight through. I felt good today and felt like I could walk forever. It wasn't long until we came to Pamplona University, a huge, lovely, state-of-the-art building. They had a sign outside saying, 'Pilgrim Passport Stamped Here', so we decided to get our passports stamped. The university itself was closed this time of year, but the security guard stamped our passports, and we were back on our heels.

On the other side of the town was a little shop and I bought some water and fruit, something to keep me going for the day ahead. I'd learned my lesson from the Pyrenees. Marc had read in his guidebook that there was a church close by and that according to most it had the best-looking stamp on the whole Camino. A large red stamp, with the name of the town surrounding a cross – and they were right, it was a lovely stamp. As Marc and I opened the door to the church, we realised it wasn't the right entrance and we were greeted by a shocked, elderly man standing there in his underpants. It was the priest and we'd walked into his living quarters. I think we'd woken him by talking outside his house, so we apologised while standing there extremely embarrassed. He stamped our credentials as quickly as he could and hurried us out of his house, but it was worth it, as the dark, blood-red stamp brings the credentials to life with its colour. He should really have had his door locked, in our defence.

Soon after leaving Cizur Menor you take a slightly nasty climb, but the views on the top are amazing. We passed through a town called Zariquiegui and met a couple of nice men walking. Their names were Johan and Christian. Johan looked homeless, with his long, grey hair and long, grey beard. But that was only because he had started walking from his doorstep, in HOLLAND and would end up walking something like 3,000km! Christian was Austrian and started in Saint-Jean. Christian was a very big guy, but a gentle giant. They seemed nice guys and we would all meet again and become better friends as the Camino continued.

After around ninety minutes of walking, Marc and I decided to stop for a cold drink in a little bar and have something to eat. I ordered what was advertised on the menu as 'Cheese and Bacon Sandwich', but in these parts of the world, bacon is not as we know it back home. The cheese was great, but the bacon was practically raw. It wasn't cooked, but apparently that's normal for this part of Spain. Not for me, sorry, so Marc gave it to the owner's dog, who loved it. Marc and I then sat outside with some orange juice and got talking to a Danish mother and daughter who were walking the Camino together. I thought they were sisters, not mother and daughter. They were both blonde and absolutely beautiful; they looked typically Danish. The daughter was called Celine and is an incredibly talented artist and could be a model in my opinion, she really is that beautiful. Celine would turn out to become a very good friend of mine during the Camino and is still someone I'm in contact with today.

After around ten minutes of having a drink and a bite to eat, Marc and I decided to get moving, leaving Celine and her mother Anna at the bar. We said our goodbyes and wished them well on the Camino, hoping we would see them again. We started moving and saw some windmills in the distance, but it seemed to take forever to get to them. There were some little hills on the way, mostly flat farm paths, though. After around a ninety-minute walk, we were walking directly under the windmills and they were pretty impressive. They were huge and very noisy, but the breeze they gave off was very welcome.

I knew we weren't very far away from one of the Camino's major landmarks now, Alto de Perdón. In the guidebook it explains that you must pass the windmills to reach Alto, so I knew we weren't far away. Reaching this point had been something I'd been very much looking forward to, after seeing it on all the Camino documentaries and movies. I felt it was going to be surreal reaching it, and it was.

Alto de Perdón is also known as 'The Hill of Forgiveness' and is at an altitude of around 800 metres. It features wrought-iron silhouettes of medieval pilgrims and horses, facing the upcoming village of Puente la Reina.

Marc and I reached the top of the hill and were in awe, we really loved it up there. The monument was erected in 1996 in honour of the hundreds and thousands of pilgrims who had walked the Camino before us. Engraved into one of the horses is *'Donde se cruza el Camino del viento con el de las estrellas'*, which translates to 'Where the path of the wind crosses that of the stars'. We had many pictures with the iron pilgrims and enjoyed an ice cream from the van parked on top of the hill. We sat and talked for around thirty minutes, watching the fellow pilgrims take photographs and take a rest, before realising we had to get moving as we had a fair way to go yet.

When you see the towns in the distance, they always seem close, but you soon realise it can be very deceiving. On a very clear day you could stand on the Hill of Forgiveness, look back into the distance and see the Pyrenees mountains in their vast glory. Today was one of those days, so I looked back at the beautiful view, said goodbye to the Pyrenees one last time and got on my way. It felt for me like the first part of my Camino was now complete. I'd walked over the French Pyrenees mountains, seen the San Fermín festival and stood at the top of the Hill of Forgiveness. To me, stage one was complete, and I was proud of it.

As we left Alto de Perdón there is a steep hill leading down to Puente la Reina, and you must be incredibly careful down here, as not also is it steep, it's full of loose rocks and is very slippery. I slightly twisted my right ankle twice going down this hill, not badly, but enough to give me about thirty minutes of pain.

We passed a town called Uterga that has a municipal and an albergue, so if you're tired, I suggest staying here. From Alto de Perdón is around a two-and-a-half-hour walk to Puente la Reina, and we were relieved when we got there as it was absolutely boiling, close to 40 degrees and approaching 2:30pm.

As we walked into town a woman handed me a leaflet about a new albergue. I wasn't going to take it, but Marc and I were soon glad I did. The leaflet had a map on the back, taking us to an albergue about a six-minute walk out of town called Albergue Santiago Apostol. It had private rooms with two beds for fifteen euros each, plus communal dinner and use of the albergue's swimming pool. Sold.

'Marc, it's got a swimming pool and private room for fifteen euros each.' I wasn't passing that up.

The main street of Puente la Reina is narrow and filled with shops and bakeries. We crossed the famous Queen's Bridge, walked up a short hill and reached the albergue, wasting no time in quickly getting changed and heading for the pool.

The Queen's Bridge was ordered to be built by Dona Mayor, wife of Sancho III. She wanted it built so the medieval pilgrims could cross the river safely. It is said that Charlemagne crossed this bridge and stayed in this town after his famous victory in the battle against the Moors. It has a population of around 2,000.

For me, this was the best albergue we'd stayed in so far. The owners were not the most welcoming people in the world, but the place was lovely, so I could ignore a bit of rudeness. After getting into our private room of two single beds, I phoned my parents and let them know I was OK. Marc was already in the pool when I got off the phone and I went outside to join him. I put my foot in the water and it was colder than ice. I expected it to be cold, but this was Eskimo standard. I decided to lie in the shade with a beer and rest my tired legs for an hour or so. Marc pointed out that I complained about the heat and then refused to get into the pool.

After I'd sunbathed and my fellow pilgrim had swum, we decided to go back into town for a decent look around. The town is a good one and has more or less everything you would need, like a post office, tourist information, shops, restaurants and a lovely church. The restaurants were all quite busy with pilgrims that night and it took us a while to find a couple of free seats. Marc and I enjoyed a pilgrim menu of bread, spaghetti, pizza, ice cream and a beer (Marc had water). All for just ten euros each, absolute bargain.

Marc and I arrived back in the albergue around 8pm and sat talking for a while, when I noticed a chess board. I love chess, my father taught me when I was a kid and I'll play any chance I get. I even beat a former chess champion of Finland once while travelling around Barcelona, a slight claim to fame. Marc and I decided to have a game and he wiped the floor with me, I didn't even get close to beating him. We were going to have another game, but Marc decided against it. He was missing his wife and children an awful lot that night and couldn't seem to focus on anything, so I suggested we go and sit outside and chat for a while.

While Marc and I were chatting, an American guy with two teenage boys sat down with us. They told us they were from a church in the United States. The oldest of the three told us he was a priest and was walking the Camino with two of his choirboys. Something didn't quite seem right with him; you know when you just get a feeling about someone? Like I said earlier, I'm a good judge of character and he seemed very strange to me, and the choirboys seemed scared to speak in front of him. Out of the blue he started asking me very personal questions like, 'Are your parents divorced?', so I began to ignore him in the hope he would go away. He then interrupted Marc and me to ask me how many women I had been with sexually, so I decided to stop him in his tracks and tell him it was none of his business and to leave us alone. Marc stood up and asked me to go inside with him. He could see I was getting angry. This guy had known me for all of five minutes and was asking me some very personal questions. I found it all very strange and part of me thinks he wasn't a priest at all. The Camino is a magical, inspiring place, but you will meet some strange folk along the way, and he was the first one for me.

A few weeks later, Marc and I would speak about this to other pilgrims who also had similar conversations with the priest. We were told that they'd flown home just eleven days into their journey across Spain, and I wasn't alone in thinking there was something very strange about him.

As I said, we had a private room with our own beds. These rooms are like cubicles and only fake walls separate you from the next room, but that's OK, it's still private enough for me. What would happen that night while we were sleeping would become one of Marc's favourite stories to tell on the Camino. He knew how much I got embarrassed by it and, while laughing his head off, he would tell everyone we met along the way.

I was in one single bed and Marc was in the other. During the night, around 2:30, I started dreaming there was a massive spider on my face.

I hate spiders!!! I can't remember any of the following, but Marc told me the following morning that I did this: I sat up in my bed and screamed at the top of my lungs, 'ARRRGGG, GET THIS FUCKING SPIDER OFF MY FACE! ARRRRGGGGG!'

I woke up the WHOLE albergue!

Marc said he jumped up out of his bed, ran over to help me and I just stared at him with no expression on my face. I then lay back down and slept like a baby until the morning. Marc couldn't get back to sleep after that and was awake all night. Sorry, Marc. While having breakfast we could hear other pilgrims talking about someone screaming and waking up the whole albergue. We just looked at each other with a knowing smile and carried on eating. The pilgrims either side of our room knew it was either me or Marc, as they asked us if everything was OK, so I explained what had happened. Every single time we met someone new, Marc would tell them this story. He thought it was the funniest thing ever, even if he didn't get any sleep.

Puente La Reina – Estella 22km

The new day took us from Puente la Reina to Estella. Both Marc and I look back on Estella fondly; it's where we both really started to enjoy the Camino and make great friends. It didn't start great for me, though, as I lost Marc and walked on the wrong track most of the way. I don't know what I did, or how I did it, but I took a wrong turn somewhere and ended up walking next to the motorway all day, on the Camino bicycle route, I think. I ended up in Estella an hour before Marc. Apparently, it's quite a common thing to do because a path forks off, and if you don't see the arrow, you're on the bike path. I thought it was strange that I didn't see any other pilgrims; I just thought they'd all left before me.

Just before I reached Estella, I came back onto the walking route and saw a medieval pilgrim hostel that's now in ruins. The walls have practically all fallen down, there is no sign of any roof and nothing at all inside. This place is a least 200 years old. There's not an awful lot left to say about the walk to Estella, because with a lot of it being motorway, I didn't really see anything worth mentioning. Marc, on the other hand, walked through farm fields and next to vineyards all day, because he walked the correct way. Estella, though, is amazing!

It has a population of around 16,000, is very busy, but also absolutely beautiful. It has banks, shops, restaurants a museum and a post office.

Estella was founded in 1909 by Sancho Ramirez. The town regularly hosts the Miguel Indurain GP, a gruelling bicycle race around Navarra. If you're tired, then it's definitely worth using up one of your rest days here if you didn't already in Pamplona. There are many albergues and finding a bed should be simple if you get into town before 3pm. Estella was the first night I'd stayed in a proper Albergue Municipal. These places are massive and fit something like 300 bunkbeds into two massive halls.

I got to town around 12:15 and the albergue didn't open until 1pm, so I sat at the start of town to wait for Marc. After around an hour, Marc came walking into town, and I explained that I accidently took the bicycle route. He thought it was funny I got lost and ended up dodging traffic all day. We found a little café to have a beer and an orange juice. After a little while, we headed to the albergue, and the queue outside was massive. It went from the front desk, all through this massive Albergue Municipal and halfway up the street outside. After about fifty minutes of being in line we were in and unpacking what we needed for the night.

After unpacking and showering, Marc and I decided to go and sit downstairs in the lobby to see if we could see anyone we knew, and lo and behold we did. Also sitting in the lobby were Anna and Celine, the Danish mother and daughter we'd met after Pamplona. We said hello and sat talking for around an hour about our last couple of days walking. They are generally fit ladies, and they found the walking pretty easy.

In some of the albergues the wi-fi isn't great. You have to walk around, and when you find a decent spot you stay there until you're done. So, I decided to check on social media and started walking around the lobby, trying to find a strong signal. I was standing in the lobby, talking to my mother on Facebook about the last few days of walking and how much I was enjoying the Camino. Celine and Anna walked past and told me they were going for a walk around town. I told them I'd see them later. I looked at Marc and saw he was speaking to a girl with a thick American accent who was looking for the wi-fi password. Apparently, they'd met a few days before – while Marc was walking ahead of me, she'd stopped him and asked him to take a picture of her.

Marc introduced me. Her name was Kim, she was 29, from Brooklyn and was extremely good-looking. She worked as a drama teacher back home and also appeared as an actress in theatre. She told the best, over-dramatic stories you will ever hear, and I could sit and listen to her for hours. Marc, Kim and I talked for a while until Kim decided to go to bed for a few hours, as she was tired after the day's walking.

Marc and I agreed on walking into town to get some food and I remember us having pasta that night and it was delicious. We later sat over a coffee and beer, talking about the nice people we'd met already and hoping we'd see more of them while walking. Marc made a prediction that Kim and I would hook up on the Camino, because he apparently sensed a spark between us. I told him not to be stupid, but Marc is far from stupid. While we were eating, Marc and I got talking to an elderly gentleman by the name of Jerry. Jerry was doing his Camino backwards, as he completed the last part of the journey the year before and was now back to complete the first stages of the walk. A very warm, kind and intelligent man who'd been a teacher, priest and author in his time, so he had plenty of stories. At this point, including the rest day in Pamplona, I'd been walking the Camino for six days. On the Camino I realised how much you can get to know somebody in a very little time. I'd been friends with Marc now for only seven days and wrote the following in my diary:

'Marc and I are in Estella; I have known him only seven days so far, but it feels much longer. When you make friends with someone on the Camino and enjoy each other's company, you tend to spend every day and night together. I walk for eight hours a day with him, and then spend all afternoon and night with him. For all that day, afternoon and night, we are constantly talking and getting to know each other. After a week it already feels that I know him just as much as people I have known back home for twenty years.'

For the people who are reading this book and have never walked the Camino, that will sound strange to you. But the people who have walked it will relate to it massively.

The next day we would walk to Los Arcos and I decided to get an early night. Marc asked Celine and Anna if they would like to walk with us and they agreed. I was hoping we would bump into Kim to also invite her, but we didn't see her again that night, so to bed we went. Ready for another day.

Estella – Los Arcos
21km

The walk from Estella to Los Arcos is so peaceful. We were only around thirty minutes into the walk, and we passed the famous wine fountain that generously gives the pilgrims free wine and water for the walk ahead, all donated by the local church and vineyard. There was a bit of a queue, with pilgrims before us wanting to fill up their bottes, so we waited, and all enjoyed a little taste of the Spanish wine made from the vineyard next to the fountain. We all filled our water bottles (with water) and got moving again.

We'd only walked a short while before the road split into two, so Marc educated me that there is also an alternate route across the mountains and not through the towns. I told Marc I would rather walk through the towns and stop at a bar, as I see enough mountains back home, and even though I love walking through that kind of terrain, I would rather see the little old Spanish towns. Marc decided to walk across the mountains, so we shook hands, wished each other luck and I hoped I'd see him again soon. You never know when you might see somebody for the last time on the Camino; an injury or a problem back home can end someone's journey in a heartbeat, and you never see them again. Every time Marc and I split up, we hoped we would see each other again.

Celine and Anna also took the route through the towns, but I soon lost them. I walked alone the whole way and I liked it a lot, as it was really the first time on the Camino I'd walked through beautiful scenery alone. I stopped and took pictures of everything, sat under a tree and took in the fresh air, talked to locals in tiny villages. That day took me way longer than it should have, but I loved it. It's what the Camino was all about for me, walking alone in a foreign country with only my thoughts to keep me company.

I stopped at a bar after a few hours of walking and sat in the sun with a cold beer. According to my map I was around three hours away from

Los Arcos. Before entering Los Arcos, I passed through a lovely little town called Cruce. It has a mix of farmlands and vineyards that stretch 9km to Los Arcos, but within this distance there is very little shade and it's extremely hot. Also, just before Cruce there's a town called Villamayor de Monjardin that has several albergues and a stunning castle, high up on a hill overlooking the town, called Castillo de San Esteban. It's now in ruins but was supposedly built in the eleventh century.

Los Arcos is picturesque, with little narrow streets and the beautiful Santa Maria church. I'd heard from a couple of fellow pilgrims that I'd met along the way that Marc was way ahead of me and had decided to keep on walking, but I was tired and decided that Los Arcos would be my final destination today. I felt a bit sad that I wouldn't have Marc's company for the night, but these things happen on the Camino, as some people are faster than others and you lose each other for a few days. I asked a little Spanish woman if she would point me in the direction of the albergue, and in very good English she told me where to go.

It was a decent enough Albergue Municipal, nothing to write home about, but it would do for a night's sleep. It was run by two men from Belgium, who were volunteers, and both of whom had completed the Camino numerous times. I can't for the life of me remember the name of the albergue, but I do remember that it cost six euros for the night and had seventy-two beds and only two bathrooms.

Marc always says one thing about the Camino: 'There are no coincidences on the Camino, when things happen, they happen for a reason.'

I believe in that also, as experiences feel more like fate than coincidence during The Way.

After a thirty-minute nap and a shower I decided to go and see more of the stunning Los Arcos. As I walked down the stairs to go outside, I heard a familiar voice asking, 'Has anybody seen Jordan? He's Welsh, wearing a bright orange Camino t-shirt and has tattoos.'

I knew that voice well. It was Marc.

Turns out the walk across the mountains had taken him a lot longer than anticipated and he hadn't walked on ahead. He was going from albergue to albergue looking for me and eventually found me. We were both happy to see each other and shared a hug before Marc got a bed in the albergue. There was only one bed left when Marc arrived and lo and behold, it was beneath me on the same bunkbed. I told Marc it was a funny coincidence that he found me, and the only bed remaining was beneath me. He told me there aren't any coincidences on the Camino, and he was right. The Camino always provides and keeps you with the people you're supposed to be with.

While Marc was getting showered, I was sitting in the albergue's reception, writing in my diary, when I noticed a young girl of maybe eighteen or nineteen sitting alone and looking very sorry for herself. I sat next to her and asked if she was OK. She told me she was suffering badly with sunburn and blisters but was otherwise OK. Her name was Skye, and she was from Pennsylvania. She was travelling alone and had never done anything like this before. I soon put my foot in it when I asked her if she was Chinese or Japanese, because she was neither. She was born in America to Korean parents and spoke fluent Korean. Sometimes my mouth works before my brain and I should have just asked where she was from, but she found my confusion funny.

Marc was soon showered and changed so we decided to tour Los Arcos. We invited Skye to join us and we all made our way into town. After an hour of exploring, Skye and I decided to have a sit down outside a café while Marc did some more sightseeing. As Skye and I were getting to know each other better, I started telling her about Kim, the girl from New York that I'd met the previous night. As I was telling Skye about Kim, I looked to my left and there she was, walking towards me. Things like that happen all the time on the Camino, it's amazing.

Skye, if I remember rightly, lived on a golf course and had quite wealthy parents. For such a small, quiet girl she wasn't afraid to travel alone, and I respected that greatly, as it couldn't have been easy. I asked Kim to join us and introduced the girls to each other. Kim had found a private hotel for a very good price on the other side of the town and was looking forward to having a full night's sleep. Both Skye and Kim had both taken the same route as me that day, through the old rustic towns, and we talked for ages about how beautiful the scenery was. Kim and Skye lived around two hours from each other (NY and PA), so they got on like a house on fire.

Marc finally re-joined us after an hour and the four of us sat talking, laughing and drinking together (Marc drinking coffee of course). The night went fast, and before we knew it, we'd downed a fair bit of San Miguel and all decide to call it a day. A hangover on the Camino is never good. As Kim was in a different hotel to us, we arranged to meet her at the edge of town at around 6am to all start walking together.

On returning to the albergue I saw a very happy, familiar face as the lovely Michele greeted us with a massive smile and a hug, before introducing us to her new friend, Carles Salvador. Carles was a very quiet man, but extremely funny. I only walked with Carles for just over a week, but I can honestly say in that week we never stopped laughing.

He was 49 and was born in Barcelona (Catalonia). I think Carles had reached a point in his life where he needed to go and find himself and get over a few things. Just four days before he started the Camino in Saint-Jean, Carles broke up with his partner of eight years. He was hiding quite a sad story from the other pilgrims, which I won't go into here, as some things must stay on the Camino. He told me they were eight happy years, but it was time to move on. I had the impression Carles was one for the ladies when he was younger, as he was on the Camino. He struck me as a kind of old rogue, and I liked that about him. In Barcelona there is a name for someone that flirts with all the girls; they call them a pirate. Carles never once called me Jordan on the Camino, it was always 'pirate'. I called him 'the old pirate' and we still refer to each other as such to this day.

So, after Michele introduced Marc and me to Carles, they agreed to join our little group of walking pilgrims and leave in the morning with us all. Marc and I talked in our beds about the new group we'd formed and how nice it was. It started with just two of us and it had grown into a little walking group. We couldn't wait for tomorrow.

By the end of the Camino I reckon Marc and I must have spoken to nearly everyone who was walking at the same time as us. We would stop somewhere for a coffee and somebody would say to us: 'Are you Marc and Jordan? I was with so and so last night, they were talking about you.'

We wouldn't have a clue who these people were, but by the end of the Camino everyone knew us.

'The tall Dutch guy who is walking with the Welsh, tattooed guy.'

That's how we were known, it was great.

Los Arcos has a population of around 1,500 people and was built by the Romans. It's a very common stop place for pilgrims to take a rest day here, due to its tranquil surroundings and cheap hotels.

Los Arcos – Logrono
28.6km

The morning came and I was woken up by pilgrims talking and hustling around the room, trying to get ready for another day of walking. Marc had been up a while before me and was downstairs having breakfast with Michele, Carles and Skye. I soon got myself ready and we were all set to go and meet Kim at the edge of town, as planned.

As Marc, Skye, Michelle, Carles and I approached Kim we noticed she wasn't standing alone and had other people with her – Anna and Celine. Fantastic, I thought, our group is now eight people, and eight people I really like. Celine and Anna had stayed in the same hotel as Kim and started talking over dinner about people they had met so far. They soon realised that we all knew each other, so Kim asked them to join us in the walking group the next morning. The eight of us all set off in high spirits, and for the first hour or so Kim and I stayed at the back of the group and enjoyed a chat while walking. Her accent was that mesmerising, it put me in a trance, so I couldn't really remember much of the first hour. She looked a dead ringer (in my opinion) for the actress Hilary Swank, so I didn't mind looking at her either.

After around 7-8km, we arrived in a small town called Torres del Rio, a lovely little town with an amazing twelfth-century church that's linked with the Knights Templar. I'd wanted to visit this town a lot, after seeing how beautiful it looked in the movie *The Way*.

(*The Way* is a movie starring Emilio Estevez and Michael Sheen, based on the Camino. If you haven't seen it, buy it immediately.)

The church here is based on the octagonal church in Jerusalem and is so peaceful. There are also a few albergues here that looked extremely nice as we passed them, and I will definitely stay here overnight on my next Camino. If you have time, please visit the church and its thirteenth-century crucifix.

We left Torres del Rio and started heading for our destination, Logrono. We had another 21km to go, so we started to get a move on. The group started to break up a bit as people became tired or stopped for breaks, but Marc and I were out in front and kept up a good pace. The walk today was mostly on natural paths and adjacent to beautiful farm fields. It was very hot and there wasn't a lot of shade, but you sucked it up and kept walking anyway.

Marc and I were now walking at a much faster pace than when we first started, and our fitness levels were rising every day due to the long walks. Soon after, we came to another town called Viana, a lively little town with a population of around 4,000. Medieval pilgrims would often stay here for a few days and shelter from the bad winter weather, and much of the town is still intact from back in the fifteenth century.

Marc and I ploughed forward and didn't take any more stops that day, passing straight through another few small towns. We arrived in Logrono around 3pm, had a coffee stop and went straight to book into the Municipal. There were thankfully plenty of beds remaining.

Logrono is quite a busy town and has a population of around 15,000, which is helped by the university here. There are bars and restaurants everywhere here and you won't struggle to stock up on essentials. If you arrive in Logrono at the end of September, you can see a festival called San Mateo. I'm pretty sure the festival is something to do with Logrono being the capital of the famous wine-growing region of La Rioja. The Parliament Square building here is impressive and was once a tobacco factory that made and distributed most of Spain's tobacco. Also, if you like tapas bars then this is the place for you.

The municipal here was very nice with great showers and comfy beds, made better by the fact no one snored very loudly during the night. Marc and I found a nice restaurant near Logrono Cathedral after showering and were joined by two pilgrims we'd met before, Johan and Christian. They sat and had a beer with us for just over an hour and it was nice to get to know them better. They were both quiet men and even though they didn't say a lot, they were very good company. They soon went back to their albergue for some sleep but were replaced by Anna, Celine, Skye and Kim. We were all starving, and the restaurant was extremely busy with pilgrims, so we decided to have a walk through town and find somewhere else to eat. We found a shop selling pizza for one euro a slice and everyone freaked out. It was the first time the girls had seen pizza since they started the Camino and the gang decided to indulge themselves.

We were all stuffed after the pizza but when we saw a frozen yogurt place, we decided we could fit a bit more in. We were all staying in the same albergue, so we decided to go and sit out in the back garden and talk the night away. It was that night, while walking around town, I realised that I liked Kim and that Marc's prediction might come true. She was so far away from the usual type of girl I go for back home, but I couldn't help but like her. She was so dorky and overdramatic that she just had this appealing personality that hooks you, and I couldn't get enough of her. I didn't really know how to tell her that, though, so I stupidly kept my mouth shut. I was talking to Anna and Celine most of the night and found them very interesting people, but it was something Kim said to Skye that grabbed my attention the most. During the discussion about the lack of men on the Camino, in front of the group Kim said, 'There aren't many good-looking men on this walk. I mean, what am I meant to do? Look at Jordan?'

I pretended that I didn't hear it and carried on talking to Celine, but secretly I was gutted, as I was starting to like the girl.

The group started to disband as the night went on and if I remember correctly, we were all in bed by 9:30-10pm that night, as we were all tired. A good afternoon all in all, but I went to bed a bit downhearted over what Kim had said. Women were the last thing I wanted on the Camino and half the reason I was here was to get away from that back home. So why was I sad about what Kim said? I liked her, I guess.

Logrono – Nájera
30.1km

The next day would take us from Logrono to Nájera, a 30.1km walk alongside main roads which then continues onto natural paths through farm fields. I had a very good night's sleep as nobody snored and I didn't wake up until 7am. That's late on the Camino. Marc had tried waking me up and I had apparently turned to him (in my sleep) and said something not so nice. Marc knew I was half asleep saying it and didn't take any offence, thankfully.

By the time I'd got ready and started walking it was around 7:35 and everyone I knew had already set off, but that was OK, I would catch up at some point. The first big town I arrived at was called Navarrete and again it is really stunning, but they all are on the Camino. The town is full of original sixteenth-century houses and has a lovely square where you can find bars and restaurants. Many of the towns on the Camino make the effort to keep their history alive by maintaining the original buildings and monuments, and I really like that about Spain. It is full of history.

You must be careful on the first half of that day's walk as you're literally walking at the side of a motorway and the cars go very fast. One slip onto the road and you could be in trouble, so please be careful.

The second half of the walk is through farm fields that have a kind of muddy, clay texture. It was fine as it was hot that day, but I imagine this would be very difficult to walk in during the winter months and the rain. Along this path I noticed there were thousands of sticks attached to a metal fence, in the shape of crosses. I was later told that pilgrims do this while walking as a sign of remembrance for deceased love ones. There are a lot of shrines like this on the Camino. I also saw a very large silhouette of a bull in the distance, high up on a hill. Not actually sure what that was for; maybe they have bullfighting there. (If you know then email me, my email address is in the back of this book.)

I stayed a while in a lovely little village called Cruce Opcion Ventosa. If I wrote it correctly in my diary, I had a beer in Café Juanka, and it was a swell little place with very helpful staff, who spoke very good English.

Around ten minutes after leaving the village is Alto de San Antón, where you will see the ruins of an early pilgrim hospital that was apparently built in the mid-sixteenth century. It's believed Roldan defeated Ferragut here by throwing a rock at him and freed the captive knights of Charlemagne's army.

After around seven hours I arrived in Nájera, an historical town and the capital of Navarre in the eleventh and twelfth centuries. Here you can visit the tomb of Dona Blanca de Castile y Navarre, the Queen of Navarre in 1156. Navarre has a population of about 8-9,000 and has many shops, restaurants and bars.

The walk that day took me seven hours and I got in around 2pm, or just after. I struggled to find the municipal at first and it turned out I had walked right past it and didn't notice. A friendly Spanish gentleman pointed me in the right direction and I finally found the municipal. My Spanish isn't great; I know some but not enough. But I can understand quite a bit, so I just listen and hope I've heard correctly.

As I walked to the municipal, I saw Marc, Kim and Skye walking towards me, and it was a welcome sight. I'd missed them that day and walking alone next to busy roads was quite boring.

The albergue didn't open until 16:30 and we had about two hours to kill. I decided to lie in the sun outside the albergue and rest my tired legs. The group all went for a drink in the bar opposite and Marc brought me a beer over. Very nice of him.

As we were standing outside, we met some more friends and we all ended up having one big room all to ourselves. The woman who ran the albergue asked us if we wanted a room with eleven beds as there were eleven of us: Marc, Kim, Skye, Celine, Anna, Johan, Christian, Carles, Michele, me and a woman Michele had met during her walk that day. I can't remember her name, but Marc and I nicknamed her the 'serial killer' – more about that soon.

We all had a communal dinner in the dining room around 6pm and it was great to be with all our new friends at the same time. Carles and I laughed and laughed as I taught him some English swearwords, while he attempted to teach me Spanish. We had pasta, salad and bread, and it was delicious. After dinner we all gathered in the municipal's seating area and talked some more. After what Kim had said about me to Skye, I decided to bring it up, because it was still bothering me a bit. If she didn't find me attractive then fine, but I found it quite a nasty thing to say in front of somebody. Kim told me she'd said it as a joke and admitted that she'd been flirting back with me since we met. I didn't know how to take that and for the sake of being made to look a fool, I told her that women were the last thing on my mind. After stupidly saying that to Kim, she seemed to back off a bit and not really talk to me for the rest of the night. I think I embarrassed her by saying I wasn't interested after she'd admitted flirting with me, but then I am an idiot at times.

Later that night Michele would come over to me and, in typical Michele style, she quietly whispered to me, 'You two have obviously got the hots for each other, you're on the Camino so let the magic happen.'

I still think about that and laugh. I miss Michele so much, even now.

I was disappointed that I'd told Kim I wasn't looking for anything on the Camino because the fact is, I thought she was beautiful. I just didn't want to look stupid. Swallowing my pride has always been my downfall, those closest to me will tell you that. Soon after I went to bed, as I felt things were becoming awkward.

Let me tell you why Marc and I nicknamed Michele's new friend 'the serial killer'. She was a nice enough woman, but extremely odd, and put the frighteners on us while we all shared the room that night. About 2am in the morning, I woke up and looked across the room to see her standing over Michele while she slept, just staring at her. I gave Marc a shake to wake him up and nodded in Michele's direction. She stood there for around five or six minutes just staring at Michele while she slept. After a while I coughed and she looked over, saw Marc and I were watching her and got back into her bed. Marc and I give each other a worried look and went back to sleep. I know calling her 'the serial killer' isn't nice, but it freaked us out. She wasn't sleep-walking, either.

Nájera has a population of around 10,000, so isn't a small place. It was under Muslim rule when built and the name Nájera is of Arabic origin, meaning 'Town between the Rocks'. The town was conquered by Ordono II of León in 923, until it was conquered by Castile in 1054 after the battle of Atapuerca.

Nájera – Santo Domingo de la Calzada 21km

Marc and I woke up at 4:30 the next morning and were out the door by 5am. I was secretly hoping Kim and Skye would still be in bed when we left, as I wanted to avoid the awkwardness of the night before, but they were up and downstairs before us. Marc invited them to walk with us and away we went.

Today was a pretty short 21km from Nájera to Santo Domingo de la Calzada, and the walk is exquisite. Most of the walk is through country tracks, passing through farmland that's so peaceful, you can literally hear every bird singing. It was amazing. We passed through a few small towns and villages, but I only stopped to buy water, as I was enjoying the

Camino so much that day. The whole walk should take me five hours and after leaving at 5am I would be in Santo Domingo by 10am, and that was way too early. I read in my guide book that the last thirty- to forty-minute walk into SD is alongside a busy main road, so I decided to find a nice quiet spot under a tree and watch the birds fly above me for an hour or two and write in my journal. I wrote the following:

'Kim and I have spoken once today, that was saying hello when we saw each other at 5am this morning. I knew it would be awkward and to be honest, it's my fault. I never have a problem saying what I think, so why didn't I tell Kim what I thought? I think I'm just reluctant to admit I like her because I came on the Camino to partly get over a woman, not to meet a new one. I am sat under a massive tree listening to the birds singing and pilgrims talking in the distance, it's beautiful. I have let Marc, Kim and Skye go on without me. I want to be alone for a while.'

Sometimes on the Camino you need moments to reflect, to sit down and go through your own thoughts for a while. Sometimes the Camino feels like a race and that's the total opposite of what it should be. I realised I needed to take more breaks and just enjoy being in the moment. The Camino is a long, sometimes gruelling experience, so you must find time to unwind. I was also confused about how I could like somebody after only a few days of knowing them. But when you spend twenty-four hours a day with someone, you get to know them very well, very quickly.

That day I walked through a town called Azofra and realised just how much of an impact the Camino has on some small towns along the route. The whole town has a population of around 400 and only survives because of the passing trade from pilgrims. It has two albergues, a small shop and a bar, but all wouldn't exist without the Camino de Santiago and the town would be more than likely abandoned. I believe there were a few hospitals here during medieval times, so the town has been accommodating pilgrims for a very long time and long may it continue.

I got into Santo Domingo at around 1pm and headed for the Albergue Casa Santo Asoc, because according to my guidebook this albergue has a chicken coop, and that sounded quite nice to me. As I walked up to the albergue I saw Marc, Kim and Skye sitting outside, and I again felt instantly awkward. I didn't come on the Camino for this and called Marc to one side so I could tell him what had happened with Kim and me.

Marc apologised for asking them to walk with us that morning, but he had no need to apologise, he wasn't to know. Kim was also Marc's friend and just because things had got a little awkward, there was no need for the group to part ways. I just wanted him to know why I was being distant.

Marc and I laughed at how we would pick the same albergue time and time again. After an hour of waiting for the albergue to open I got changed, showered and made my way outside to see the chickens. I ended up falling asleep on the grass outside and woke up to find Michele, Kim and Skye sitting opposite me, talking to each other. I sat up and started talking to Michele about her day, and she told me Carles was running late. His legs were hurting him and he said he might stop at a small town just before Santo Domingo.

I turned to Kim and asked her how her day had been, and she totally blanked me and began to talk to Skye. That, to me, was Kim's way of basically telling me to **** off, so I did. I found Marc upstairs in the dorm and told him I didn't want to walk with them anymore as I didn't need this kind of thing on the Camino. There is enough drama in your everyday life, and I didn't want it here, in what should be a stress-free experience. He agreed and we decided to walk alone in the morning, just me and him. Looking back now Kim and I should have just been honest with each other. We wasted days not talking and regretted it by the end of the Camino. I blame myself, though. It's the idiot inside of me.

Santo Domingo is a quiet town of around 7,000 and is named after Saint Dominic, who dedicated his life to improving the Camino for pilgrims and built many of the bridges and roads that are used by pilgrims today. He also built a pilgrim hospital that's now a very big hotel. If you have time, visit the museum and cathedral. They're both deep in history and are beautiful.

There is a chicken coop in the cathedral that comes with a fascinating tale called 'Miracle of the Coop' that has become a famous story on the Camino. According to legend, a pilgrim couple and their son stopped at an inn here on their way to Santiago and the innkeeper's daughter took a shine to the son. After he rejected her advances, she hid a silver goblet in his backpack and reported him to her father for stealing it, leading to the innocent boy being captured and hanged for theft. The parents had left before him that morning and were oblivious to what had happened.

The parents reached Santiago and began to worry, as he hadn't caught up with them, so they retraced their steps, hoping to find him. On returning to Santo Domingo they were horrified to see their son hanging on the gallows, but miraculously he was still alive. The parents rushed to the sheriff's house to tell him, interrupting his dinner. The sheriff replied, 'Your son is no more alive than the cooked chicken on my plate,' which led to the chicken jumping off the plate, alive and well. The sheriff, believing he had witnessed a miracle, ran to the gallows to cut down the innocent lad, who was given a full pardon and set free.

Make of that what you will.

It was in Santo Domingo that Marc and I met Mauricio Longo, another pilgrim who would become part of what I call my 'Camino Family'. Mauricio was a very quiet but suave Italian man and, like Marc, is one of the most genuine, kind souls that I met during the 600 miles. Marc, Mauricio and I have all met up in London, Brussels, Holland and the Ukraine after the Camino, and they are both now two of my closest friends in life.

Marc and I were sitting outside a bar that had an albergue opposite when Mauricio walked towards us with Jerry, a pilgrim I'd met a few days before. Mauricio had started his Camino from Saint-Jean, but this was the first time we'd bumped into him. He'd worked in a bank for many years but felt a bit disillusioned with life and wanted 'to be free', as he put it. The bank he worked in was making people redundant and he volunteered, so with a payoff and a love for travel, he was on the Camino. Mauricio was definitely a ladies' man and was quite the charmer and I liked that, the stereotypical Italian man.

We all had dinner together and all hit it off with him straight away. Looking back, I wish Marc and I could have met Mauricio at the start of the walk and shared the entire journey together.

Along with meeting new friends that night, Marc and I both received an email from Fritz and sadly, it wasn't very good news at all. Fritz's wife had been taken very seriously ill back home in Holland and he had left the Camino immediately to be with her. Marc and I were absolutely saddened for Fritz and his wife, as we both knew how badly he wanted to accomplish the task of the Camino, but his family came first, as they do with us all. We both responded to his email and wished him and his wife well, before raising a toast to them.

A while later Marc, Mauricio, Jerry and I were joined by Kim, Skye, Johan, Christian, Anna and Celine. Marc asked me if I wanted to leave but I refused. I wasn't going to spoil my evening because Kim and I were too stubborn to talk. We all had dinner together and all took turns to explain what we were enjoying most about the Camino. There is so much positive energy in being surrounded by people who share your interests and are going through the same emotions as you, on what truly is a gruelling walk at times. It's nice to hear different people's thoughts and feelings on the Camino and know you're not the only one that struggles at times or is missing home and needs to be alone.

Kim and I still didn't talk, and after a while, it was that time of night again to hit the sack. We arranged to walk with Mauricio and Jerry the next day and meet them outside their albergue at 5:30, as their albergue was on the edge of town and we had to walk past it anyway.

I didn't sleep well that night. I don't think anyone did, as Christian was in our dorm and believe me, that man can snore. He woke up everyone at some point during the night and nobody had a decent night's sleep. I threw one of my flip-flops at him during the night and it hit him straight between the eyes. He didn't even flinch. As planned, though, we were up and ready by 5:15 and on our way to meet our new friends. Jerry and Mauricio were waiting for us outside their albergue, like they said they would be, and we all started walking. It was cold that morning and that came as a very welcome bonus for me. I walked in my t-shirt while everyone put on their jackets. I'd been waiting for a cold/rainy day for a few days now as I needed to cool down.

Santo Domingo de la Calzada – Belorado 23km

The walk today was 23km and again we left a lot earlier than we really needed too. The historic roads of the Camino today would take us from Santo Domingo to Belorado, but they started off not so historic. The first half of the journey took us back to the main road of the N-120, the motorway we'd walked on a couple of days ago. You must keep an eye out for the yellow arrows, because if you miss one, you could end up walking all the way to Belorado via the N-120. But around halfway through the walk, you turn off the road and walk on a quiet path.

We didn't stop walking that day until we reached a very small town called Villamayor del Rio with a population of no more than fifty people. The bar there was open, and I soon found out that Mauricio liked to have a beer just as much as me. We sat there for around an hour and had something to eat while passing some time away.

Belorado was around 5-6km away from here and we'd made very good time, so we decided to walk slowly and not kill ourselves too much when we didn't need to. We could have walked a further distance most days, but I didn't see the point. I had all the time in the world so why rush it? We passed a few more villages and had a beer in every single one.

Marc and I ended up in front of Mauricio and soon started walking with a girl called Quinn and, like Kim, she was also from Brooklyn. She was a lovely girl and gave Marc and me a rubber bracelet each, to keep us going on the Camino. The bracelet had a love heart and a pair of feet engraved into it.

'You have to follow your heart and keep walking,' she told us. A lovely gift from a complete stranger, that sums up Camino life. We would keep bumping into Quinn across the Camino and it was always lovely seeing her. She was also a very attractive girl. Her brother was one of the writers for a show called *Saving Hope* over in the States and it was in its fifth or sixth season, a pretty big show over there.

As you arrive in Belorado you're walking on a farm path that is right next to the motorway. You're a lot safer here, but the noise of the traffic isn't very nice, but you take the rough with the smooth. Belorado, on the other hand, is a quiet, slow-moving and peaceful town. I noticed that everyone that lived there was all elderly, and I didn't really see any young locals at all. It really is peaceful. There is a stunning medieval arcade that's filled with shops, bars, restaurants and a bank, so you shouldn't have any trouble stocking up or getting more money. There's an old castle ruins that I don't know much about, but it's lovely to look at.

Marc's Dutch guidebook told us that there was an albergue here with a swimming pool, and we headed straight for it. We got a bed and unpacked and noticed Anna and Celine also unpacking, so we all hugged and said hello. We then decided to go and check out the pool, as it was very hot at this point, and the four of us ended up playing water polo for well over an hour.

Anna and Marc decided they wanted to stop, as they wanted to try the free yoga session that was being offered next to the pool. We all got out and I took great satisfaction in laughing at Marc being the only man out of the fifteen people participating. Jerry and Mauricio soon joined us after getting the last of the beds. I remember not being hungry that night and I sat by the pool writing in my diary while Marc, Anna, Celine, Jerry and Mauricio all had dinner in the albergue restaurant. The game of water polo, a day's walking and the Spanish heat really tired me out by around 18:30, so I went for a nap. I didn't rise again until the next morning.

Belorado – Ages
28km

I don't know why, as I went to bed early enough, but I just couldn't wake up the following morning. Marc, Mauricio, Jerry, Anna and Celine all left without me and I finally got up at 7:30. On starting to leave Belorado, I heard a voice call me from behind and it was Skye. She'd also woken up late, so we started walking together. We were heading to San Juan de Ortega, which was 25km away, and the walk included some very steep climbs, reaching some 1,150 metres above sea level. There isn't much shade, and some parts are strenuous but take it slow and you'll really enjoy it.

We didn't stop walking that day until we reached Villafranca de Montes de Oca, where we stopped at a café for Skye to put on some cream, because she had some very bad sunburn. After around thirty minutes or so, we started walking, and the next part was extremely steep. The sun was burning, and gallons of sweat were pouring off me. Our pace had slowed but we fought on and headed towards San Juan de Ortega but got totally lost. I hadn't got lost on the Camino yet. I'd taken a wrong turn, but not lost. We ended up in a town called Ages, about 5km past San Juan. I don't know how we did it, we just must have switched off for a second and not seen an arrow.

Skye and I spoke about staying in Ages together but decided, as Marc and the group were in San Juan, we'd walk the 5km back, to be with them. I went straight to the one albergue that was there, and Marc and Mauricio were standing in reception, not looking very happy.

Marc looked at me and said, 'This albergue is full and the next one is in Ages; we have to start walking again.'

Skye and I couldn't believe it; we were just there and were heartbroken, to say the least. We couldn't believe we had to walk back to the town we'd just come from. It really did feel like torture but turned out to be for the best, as there were four albergues and all had plenty of beds spare. That last 5km walking back took me and Skye ninety minutes, where usually 5km would take us around fifty minutes.

When we got back there, Skye and I slept for around forty minutes before waking up and deciding to get some food. We found Marc downstairs and he joined us, telling Skye and me that during his walk that day he'd come across a girl who'd fallen heavily down some church steps. He'd walked with her for over an hour to make sure she was OK. That's the kind of guy Marc is, he will always help others before himself.

Later we were joined by Celine and Anna, who also had to walk to Ages after not finding a bed in the earlier town. After food, Anna and Marc had a walk around the small village and I went upstairs to relax. Celine came with me and kindly gave me a shoulder massage, as they were aching that day, so I repaid the favour by sewing a hole in her favourite top, which she'd accidentally ripped.

I hadn't noticed, as she must have got to the albergue before me, but Kim walked past me while I was sewing Celine's top and got into the bed straight opposite mine. She lay down on her bed and we kept catching each other's line of sight and it felt awkward, so I decided that I couldn't let it carry on like this. When I finished sewing, I went to try to clear the air by asking if we could be friends again. I told her I was sorry if I'd come across as a dick, that wasn't my intention and that I liked her company. She also apologised, so we hugged and went downstairs for a chat. We spent the rest of the night together until about 11pm, talking about our love for the TV show *The Office* U.S. and having a great laugh, until we decided we should probably get to bed.

I felt a weight had been lifted off my shoulders, going to bed knowing that Kim and I had become friends again. I hate arguing with people and haven't got time for it. It plays on my mind for weeks afterwards and gets to me. But the argument I had with a Korean gentleman during this night in Ages wasn't one of those times. Walking at the same time as us were a group of Korean students and they didn't have the same pilgrim spirit as the rest of us. Skye, who can speak fluent Korean, would overhear the group talking and informed us that they were calling us names and saying bad things about us. The group in question had a teenage boy with them and they would make him RUN the Camino and order him to buy ten beds in the albergue for when they got there. That shouldn't be allowed, in my opinion, but it's made worse by some albergue owners letting them get away with it. If I didn't have a bed, I'd keep walking until I found one, and that's the way it should be.

That night in Ages I just couldn't keep my cool. It was just after 1am in the morning and everyone was asleep in a dorm of around thirty beds. A phone rang very loudly and woke up most people in the dorm. Now it's 1am and people are waking up in a few hours. You'd have thought he'd have turned his phone off. Instead of doing the civilised thing, he answered the phone and starts talking Korean as loudly as he possibly could. I thought he might have been telling someone to ring back as it was 1am, but he just kept talking and talking and talking. A few people were getting angry in the dorm and were giving him the 'shh' treatment, but it wasn't working, and it had been about three minutes of him basically screaming into his phone. After already being wound up about them calling us names earlier in the day I got out of bed, stormed over to him and shouted, 'Shut the fuck up, people are trying to sleep!' in his face. He ended the call and turned his phone off. Am I proud of it now when looking back? Absolutely! Just a clear lack of respect for everyone in the room and I have no time for it. Even if it was an emergency back home, he still could have walked outside to answer the call. Most Korean people I met on the Camino were lovely, it was just this annoying group that wound everybody up.

After a night of broken sleep, I woke up around 6am and found everyone in the dorm had already gone, but I decided it was a good thing, as I could walk and write in my diary without distraction. I think I needed a bit of a break as well, because even though I loved the new friends I'd made, it's also nice to walk alone sometimes and gather your thoughts.

The cobbled streets of St Jean sit underneath the Pyrenees mountains.

A long way to go.

San Fermin – Running of the bulls

Alto del Perdon

— 60 —

61

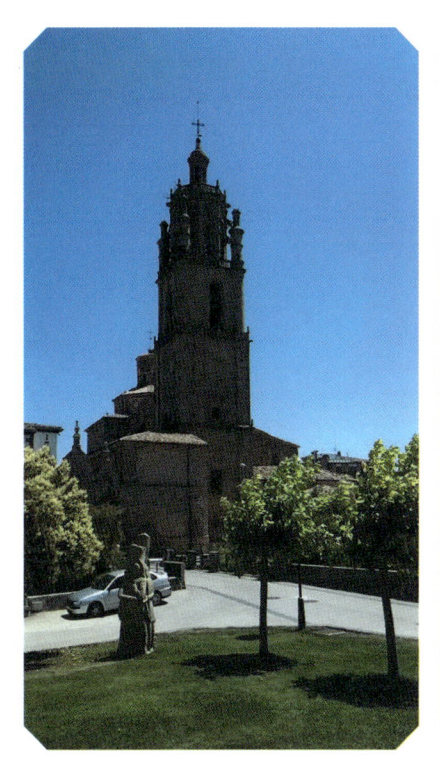

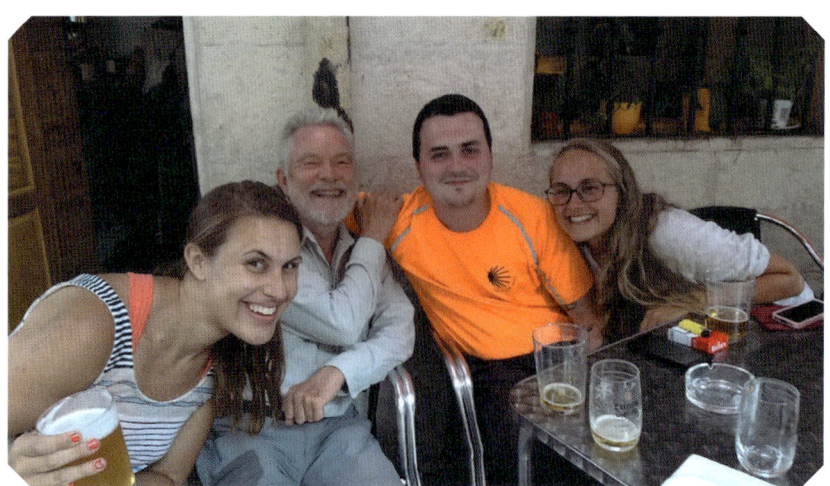

An evening with new friends.

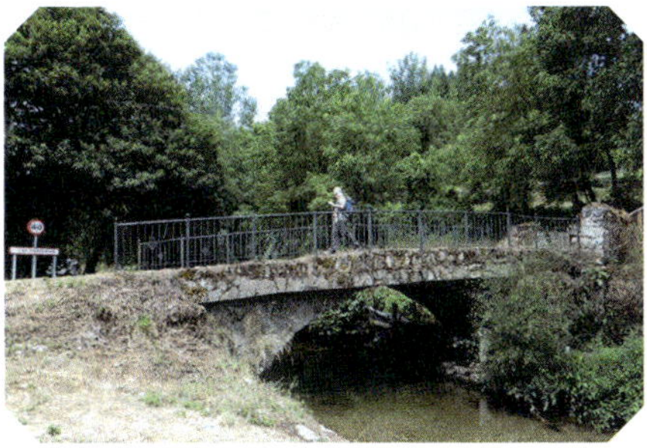

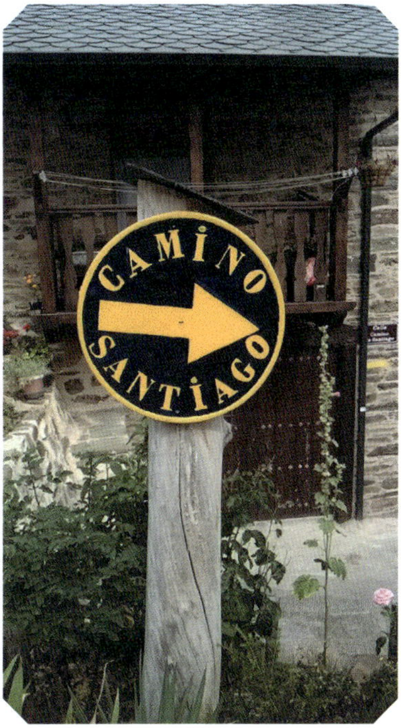
CAMINO
SANTIAGO

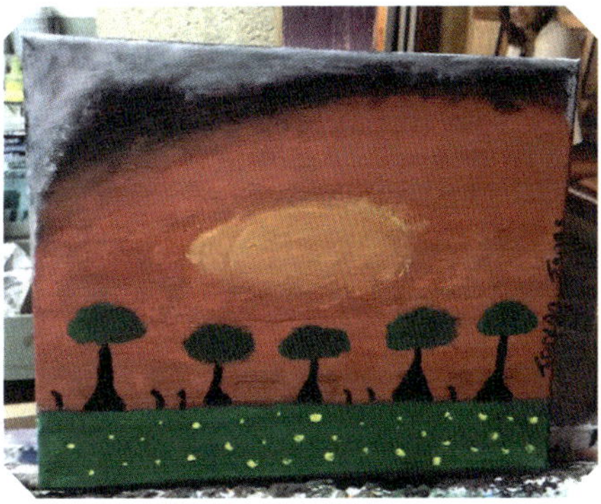

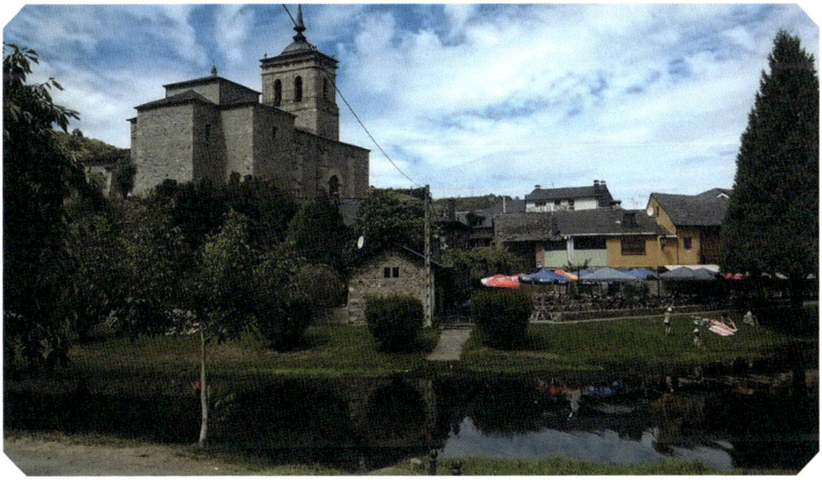

Cruz de Ferro

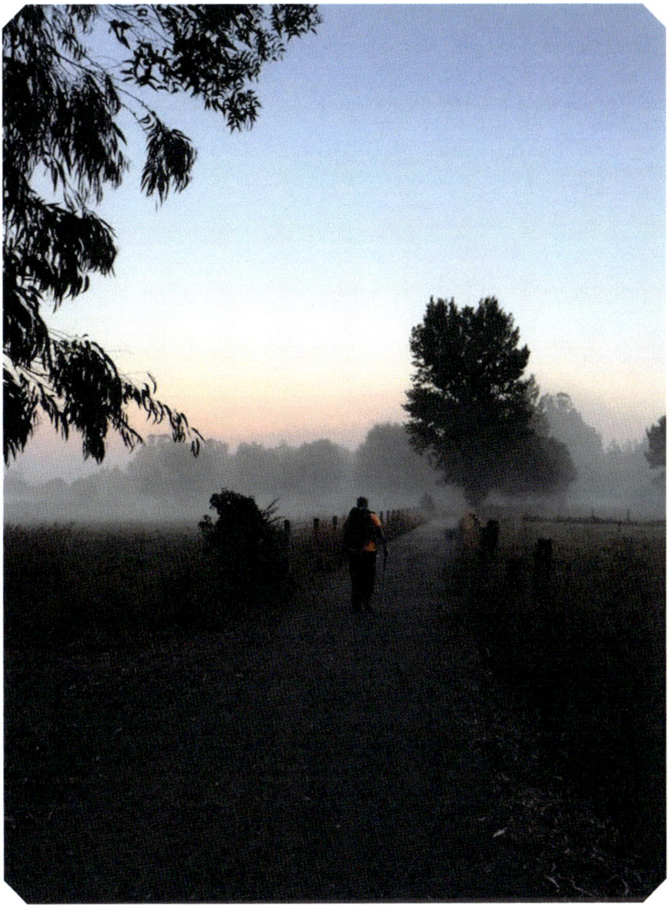

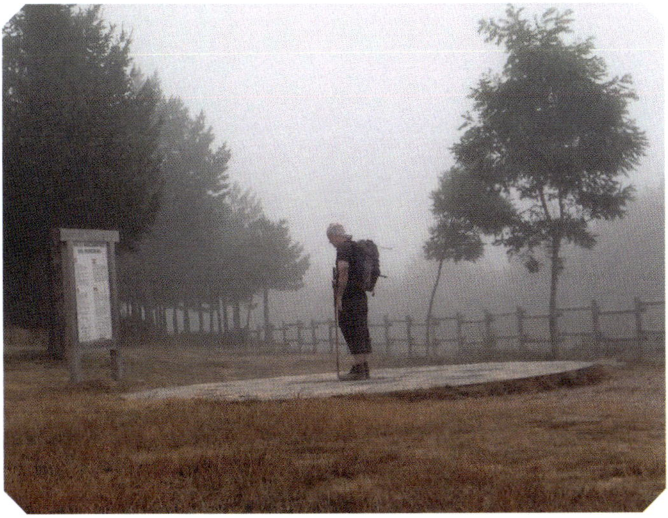

The fog clearing as Marc approached Cruz de Ferro

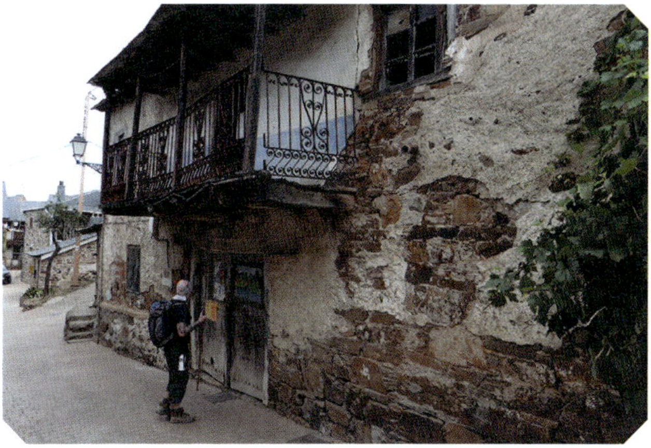

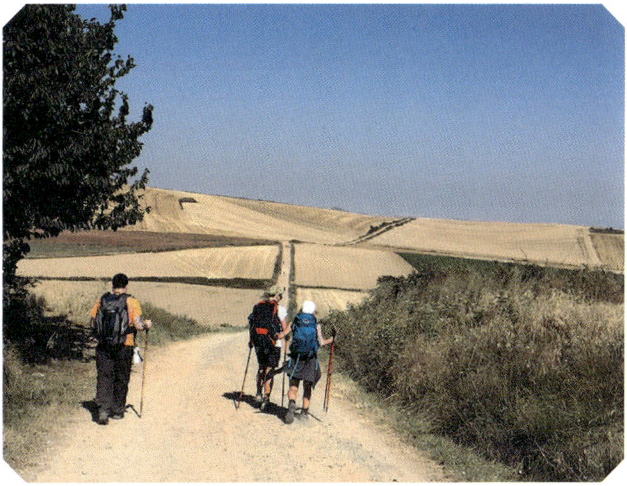

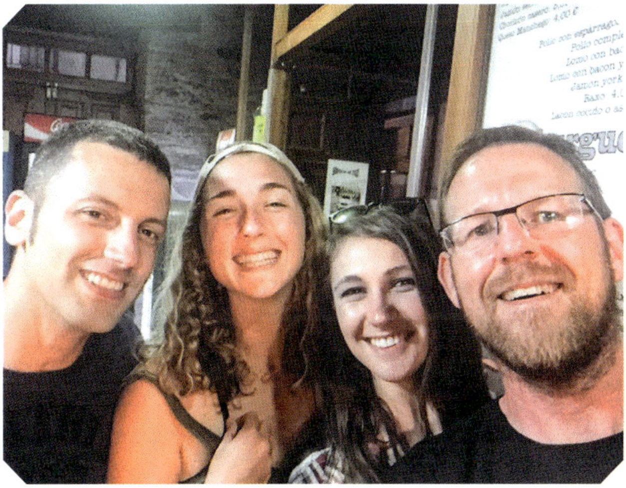

Michelle, Marc, Mauricio, Kim, Anna and Celine

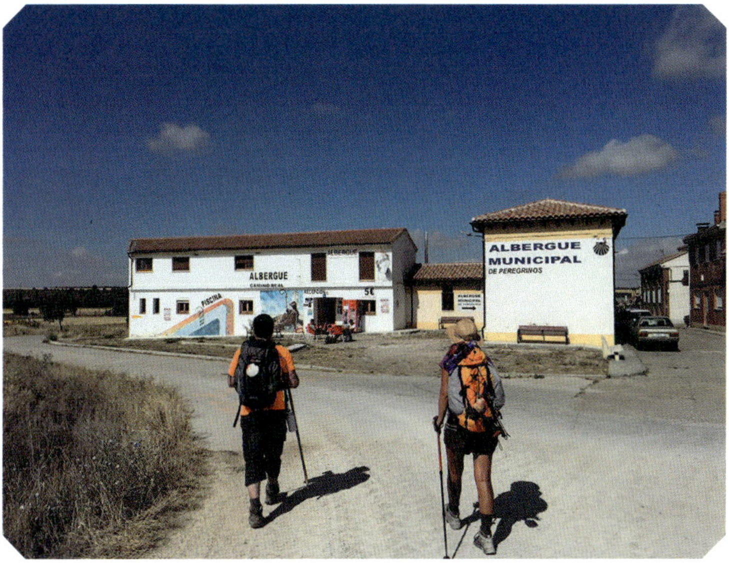
ALBERGUE
PISCINA
5€
ALBERGUE
MUNICIPAL
DE PEREGRINOS

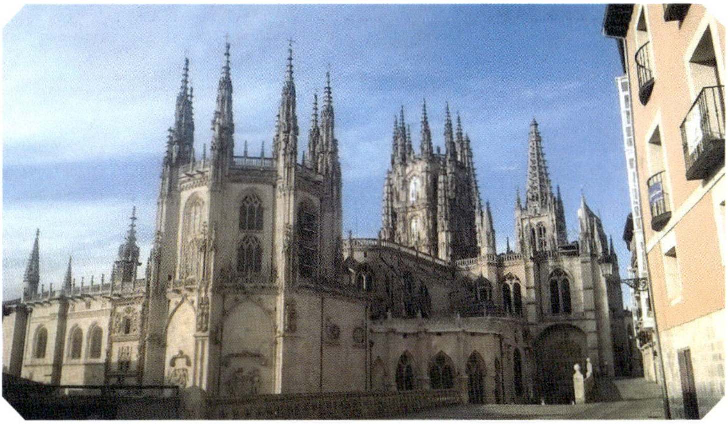

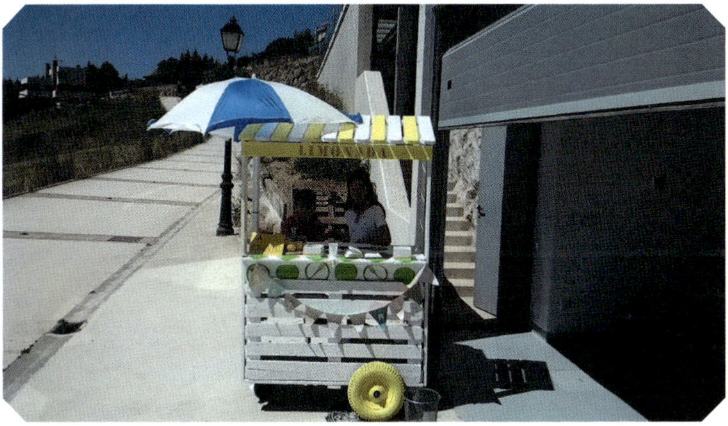

70

— 71 —

Getting closer

Santiago de Compostela

The last supper

The end – at the cliffs of Finisterre

Muxia – 612 miles away from where we started

My parents and I back in Santiago with Marc – 2017

Marc and I back on the Camino – 2018.
It's in our blood now, it always brings us back.

Ages – Burgos
24km

The walk starts along a quiet path through an oak forest, before passing through a valley and descending into Burgos. During the walk today you come across a town called Atapuerca, where you can take a 3km detour off route to visit the archaeological site of the earliest known human remains. In the year 2000, UNESCO declared this a World Heritage Site. The remains of 900,000-year-old humans were found, giving the world far more insight into the evolution of human beings. The dig is still ongoing as they hope to uncover more, maybe older remains.

It's a hard slog walking into Burgos. There are a lot of people to get past, as this is a major city, but Burgos was and will always remain a special place to me. I know I say that different towns/villages are beautiful, but you have seen NOTHING until you see Burgos! I don't want to give much away, because you have to see it for yourself, but Burgos Cathedral is… I can't put it into words.

It was built in the thirteenth century and is one of Spain's biggest cathedrals. It was originally Gothic and has been modified by some amazing architects over the years, giving it different designs and carvings all the way around. It isn't the kind of cathedral you can go in for some peace and quiet; the tourists here are forever packing the place out. Seriously though, it's one of the most beautiful, extravagant, mesmerising buildings you will ever see. Burgos as a city is just as wonderful and is bursting with life, unsurprising as its population is between 180,000 and 200,000. Everything you could want is in Burgos and you'll want to stay there two days to see it all; that's my opinion, anyway. You can catch a tour train that drives around the city, showing all the sites and important places.

As I arrived at Burgos, I headed for the Municipal La Casa del Cubo, which has 150 beds spread across four floors, and the place is huge. As I walked inside, I noticed Marc and Mauricio waving at me, so I went to say hello and found it funny we'd picked the same albergue as each other yet again. Jerry then walked in. We all gave him a loud round of applause as we knew today was his last destination. We shook his hand and let him know we were proud of him, as he'd completed the Camino his way and he should be very proud. He did it backwards, but he still did it.

A little while later the four of us were sitting in the bar opposite with a bottle of water each, when we saw a group of pilgrims walking up the hill towards La Casa with beaming smiles all over their faces. Skye, Anna, Celine, Michele, Carles, Johan, Christian and Kim had all found each other that day and were coming towards us like a bunch of hyperactive teenagers, and it was a fantastic thing to see. Marc and I would get excited when we used to see pilgrims we knew, and it's a brilliant feeling when they get excited at seeing you in return. We all hugged and said hello to each other and agreed to meet back by this same bar in one hour, after everyone had been assigned a bed and showered. Luckily there were enough beds in our albergue for them all, so we decided to have a proper drink and wait for them all at the bar.

Marc, Mauricio, Jerry and I were sinking them back quite fast. Jerry was drinking jugs of sangria and had three in the first hour. It was his last night and he was letting his hair down, I loved it.

Soon after, the whole gang was outside and there were twelve of us all having the time of our lives. We were sitting in a beautiful part of Spain, with complete strangers who felt like family, drinking and reminiscing like we'd all known each other years. It really was heart-warming. We were even joined by some locals at one point who wanted to 'party' with us, but I'm pretty sure they were just after the women.

Later in the night we all took it in turns to say a few words to Jerry and wish him well in life after the Camino. He didn't give any feelings away, but I knew it touched him. Kim had sat next to me all night and as the drink started to flow faster and faster, the more we flirted, and I think we both wanted to make a move on each other. We all continued eating, drinking, telling stories and laughing until around 10:15, when we decided that most of us were drunk and absolutely shattered. Marc even drank a glass of sangria that night. I couldn't believe my eyes. It was only Kim, Marc, Mauricio and myself still outside and I decided to walk Kim to her dorm. Marc stayed behind to see if Mauricio was OK, as he'd had quite a bit to drink. I offered to walk her to her bed and realised that it wasn't that far from my bed in the same dorm.

As she gave me a hug goodnight and was getting into bed, I pulled her back and said, 'I promised myself that when I came on the Camino,

I wouldn't let anything happen with any women. I didn't even want to look at a woman. I needed to get away from all that and be on my own. But that all changed the moment I set eyes on you.'

I still say to this day, that was the most romantic thing I have ever said to anybody in my entire life and probably ever will be. Kim really didn't expect me to just admit that and come straight out with it. But I was glad I did when she told me she liked me, kissed me on the cheek and told me she would see me in the morning. That was until she climbed into my bed an hour later in just her underwear …

You can probably guess what happened next.

You have this idea in your head of what the Camino will be like before you go and I guarantee you, it will be nothing like reality. In no way, shape or form did I go on the Camino to meet anybody. That was the last thing on my mind, but it happened, was part of my Camino and I wouldn't change any of it for the world. Kim ended up falling asleep in my bed, but I woke her up soon after, as I didn't want people waking up at 5am and seeing Kim in my bed. I wouldn't want her to be embarrassed if she woke up and saw people staring at us.

I woke up at 6am and looked across at Kim, who was sitting on her bed and was the only one left in the dorm, as everyone else had gone. We went downstairs to see if we could find anyone and luckily our entire group was standing in reception. We saw Jerry getting ready to leave and all hugged him goodbye. It was sad to see one of us going home.

Kim, Marc and I had decided to have a rest day in Burgos and go sightseeing for the day. We asked the others to join us, but I got told two bits of bad news. Michele informed us that Carles was having so much pain in his legs that he'd got up before us all and made his way to the train station to return to Barcelona. It's never nice when someone must leave; it's heart-breaking for the person and for their friends who have to continue without them. I was as gutted for Carles as I was for Fritz, but Carles and I have remained great friends and we talk nearly every day over the internet since I returned home.

The second bit of bad news was that Kim had been developing very nasty blisters over the last few days and was planning on catching a bus to Sahagún after the rest day and would start walking from there. Her feet were really bad, and she didn't want to walk the dreaded Meseta (a barren piece of land that stretches nearly 220km) in so much pain. That would mean Kim would be six or seven days in front of us and there would be no way of me catching up. Marc and I were quick but not that quick. I knew that by the time I got to Santiago she would be already home in Brooklyn, and that didn't feel right to me. It didn't to her either. But she couldn't walk the whole way with the state her feet were in and it would have taken her weeks and weeks to get to the end. She didn't have that much time, she had to take the bus and that was it.

Practically everyone ended up having a rest day in Burgos and we had a great day sightseeing. Burgos is a busy place and so full of life, so Kim and I sat for a while and watched the world go by together. It felt like I had known her years. A group of Spanish schoolchildren from Madrid were on a school trip to meet pilgrims and they approached Kim and me as we were sitting down with a coffee. We must have looked like typical pilgrims, because we didn't have any of our walking gear on. One of the children asked me if I could give him something from the Camino, to take back to Madrid and display in his classroom. I gave him the bracelet Quinn had given to me and made him promise to look after it for me while I wrote my email address down on his clipboard. A few weeks after returning home from the Camino I received an email from the child's teacher, explaining that he had won the competition for getting the best item from a pilgrim and he shows it to everyone that walks into the classroom. She said he was extremely proud of it, and that made me smile. That's what life on the Camino is about. I hope he's still got it and is looking after it for me.

We had another night in the same albergue and again Kim and I shared a bed, away from the other pilgrims this time. Standing in the reception the next morning, Kim could hardly walk because of the blisters on her feet. Everyone decided to start walking, but I couldn't go with them. I know myself, and if I'd walked and left Kim behind, I would have felt horrible, and I genuinely would have missed her. That's very strange for me to feel like that, but I couldn't ignore it.

I told Marc and the others I needed time to think about what I was going to do and if I was going to walk and catch them up or go with Kim days ahead. Marc told me that this was my Camino, and I should do what I thought was right, but also told me that if I skipped some of the Camino, I would regret it. I let the group leave without me and stayed with Kim, the hardest decision I had to make on the Camino.

Kim and I had a few hours to spare while waiting for the bus to Sahagún and we sat in the big Burgos square talking and admiring the cathedral. I was starting to doubt whether I'd made the correct decision and Kim picked up on it. She could tell just by looking at me that I was confused. She told me that she was going to take the bus to Sahagún alone and that I was going to catch up with Marc by foot. Her words were, 'You came to Spain to walk the Camino. This is a once in a lifetime thing. You need to go and walk it. You'll regret it if you don't,' and she was right. The longer I sat there waiting for the bus, the more I realised I was making the wrong decision. I thought the absolute world of Kim and I always will, but I knew in my heart that I had to carry on with my Camino. It wouldn't have felt right if I'd got on that bus. I told her how sorry I was that I couldn't go with her, as much as I wanted to. We were both gutted, but both knew it was the right thing for me to do.

I walked her to the bus stop, waited with her for the bus to arrive and watched her leave. Knowing that was the last time I was probably going to see her was sad. I wish we'd spent more time together on the Camino and regretted the few days we spent not talking and that was my fault entirely, but that's life, you learn from it.

But luckily fate wasn't done with me and Kim yet. More on that later.

Burgos is the historic capital of Castile and was founded in the year 884. It has been the scene of many wars: with the Moors, the struggles between León and Navarre, and between Castile and Aragon. Castilian nobleman and military leader El Cid Campeador is buried in the grounds of Burgos Cathedral, as he was born a couple of kilometres north of Burgos and was raised and educated there.

Burgos – Tardajos
12km

I knew I was around three hours behind everyone else and hoped they stopped at a few bars at some point, as that would give me enough time to catch up. After around ninety minutes of walking I texted Marc to see where he was and tell him I'd decided to keep walking after all. He was relieved and told me I'd made the right choice. He would wait for me in a town called Tardajos and according to my guidebook I was around one hour away.

As I was walked into town, I saw he was sitting outside a bar waiting for me. That was when the Camino gave us another sign. A few days before, I'd found a business card on the floor, picked it up and saw it was advertising an albergue, so I gave it to Marc. As I sat down at the table next to him, we shook hands and he told me I'd made the right choice to keep walking, and I agreed.

Marc opened his guidebook to see where we should continue walking and the business card fell out. As he picked it up, he realised that we were sitting opposite the albergue advertised on the card. It was an uncanny coincidence and Marc took it as a sign we should stay there. We hadn't walked far, only 12km in fact, but we both believe in fate, so I agreed, and it turned out to be the nicest albergue of the whole Camino. A newly renovated building that was a four-star hotel and doubled up as an albergue. The man who owned it was lovely enough to give us one of the hotel rooms for the price of a pilgrim bed as we were the only ones there; a lovely gesture and Marc and I didn't hesitate to bite his hand off. A massive room with two single beds and the best air con around. The room had one of those amazing showers that spray water from the bottom of the shower right to the top. I think Marc and I both showered for over forty minutes each, it was that good

After we'd showered, we decided to eat. I asked the nice man who upgraded our room if there was any steak available in the restaurant and was told two pieces would be with us shortly. He left the front desk and walked us into the restaurant, where he showed us to our seats and poured us some water and gave us a basket of bread. Typical Spain. A little while later he came out with two plates and we couldn't believe our eyes at the size of these steaks. They were incredible and were sitting with a huge pile of fries each. Marc and I looked in disbelief and wondered how much this was going to cost. We didn't mind, but we didn't want another Pamplona situation. If I'd eaten that meal in Cardiff I know for a fact, just because of the size of the steak, it would have cost me £50 at least.

Marc and I finished eating and asked for the bill, to which the hotel owner/cook replied, 'No there's no bill needed, just give me three euros each.' We asked him if we'd heard him correctly and he told us, 'The money doesn't matter to me, my friends, and as long as you have a good meal, that's what matters. You pilgrims need to keep your strength up and the steak needed using today and would have been thrown out, so you pay me for the fries and bread only, so three euros each will be fine'. He really didn't have to do that and we both know that kind man lost money giving us that meal for just three euros each, but that summed up how nice people are on the Camino. There are a lot of horrible people in this world, but there's an equal number of people who are kind-hearted and genuinely lovely. Marc and I felt bad just paying six euros in total, but he wouldn't take any more money, so we had to listen to him.

We thanked him and went outside in the sun for a few beers, buying them from the vending machine by reception. I put in three extra euros but took no beer, so at least he could have some of the money back that he let us off.

We sat outside and talked way into the night. I even think Marc had a beer that night, which is a rare occasion, and around 9pm we decided to hit the sack. As we were walking back to the room I remembered Marc had left the window open and prayed the room hadn't been overrun by flies (he tells people that it was me that left the window open, but it wasn't). If you leave a window open in Spain, flies take over the room. It's a well-known fact and it's exactly what happened. There must have been a hundred of them, and that's not an exaggeration. It took Marc and me over an hour to try and get them all back out of the window. Trying to direct them with pillows or hitting them with a rolled-up guidebook. We'd turn the lights off to try and sleep and a fly would buzz by one of our ears, so it was light back on and back to chasing it around the room. We finally got to sleep and I heard Marc's alarm go off around 5:30. He got straight up and ready to go, but I fell back to sleep, so he went on without me and I started walking about 7am, as the bed was just too comfy.

Tardajos to Hontanas
21km

When leaving Tardajos you pass some *refugios* and a little fountain before a steep climb to the top of a hill, where you're greeted with a wonderous sight. As far as the eye can see is just a flat, desert-like landscape, with not a single tree or building in sight, but stunningly, magnificently beautiful all the same.

For many the Meseta is somewhat of a nightmare and a lot of people skip this part of the Camino, but not me. Spain is one of the most mountainous countries in Europe, but don't let that fool you, because the Meseta covers over 40 percent of Spain's land mass. It's a desert-like environment with no trees or buildings to keep you shaded, and I was about to start walking 220km across the barren land. It is extremely hot during the summer and absolutely freezing in winter, which makes walking it quite dangerous. Many people each year have to be rescued by the emergency services as the heat gets too much and people collapse. If you walk far enough each day you can reach an albergue, but many people sleep rough as the heat slows them down, and they set up camp on one of the many deserted, dried-up fields.

The Meseta for me was something I'd been really looking forward too. It's known as the time for reflection on the Camino, where people have endless opportunities to think about their lives and work out any problems they may have at home. I stood staring down over the vast nothing for a few minutes, taken aback by how big and beautiful it is. You look ahead as far as the eye can see and you realise that at some point over the coming weeks, you're going to walk across it all, but it's a bit daunting, an amazing feeling. All the worries I had in Saint-Jean were now long gone and I knew I was going to love every minute of this gruelling next stage.

I continued walking and came to a town called Hornillos del Camino which has another old, Gothic church, but there is nothing else here. A bit further on, after around 4km, you come to an albergue in the middle of nowhere that's run by hippy volunteers. They were sitting outside playing loud music and looking to be loving life, but I gave them a wave and kept walking. I walked a while further across the barren land and soon came across a town that remains one of my favourite places in the whole world: Hontanas. I fell in love with many towns and cities on the Camino, but Hontanas is one place I will always truly love and will visit again. You're walking slightly uphill and as you reach the top, you're looking down on a tiny little town built in the middle of nowhere. There must be only thirty buildings in the whole town, it's amazing. If I ever want to move away and never be bothered again, this is where I'll come.

I'd noticed that during the last thirty minutes of walking, I'd become quite dizzy and felt a bit sick. After I'd sat a while at the top of the town, I realised that I was burning up and had a bit of sunstroke. People on the Camino have been put out of action for days and days with sunstroke, and I really didn't want that to happen to me. I'm not stupid, I know my limits, and I decided I was going to have to cut today short, but I'd walked around 21km anyway.

I wasn't risking walking further and getting more ill, so I picked Albergue El Puntido, because it had a nice bar, looked very welcoming and was cheap at only five euros. It was still relatively early and was around 13:30 when I was showered and settled in, but I felt ill from all the sun, so I decided there was only one thing to do – grab a beer and sit in the shade all day. I knew that stopping early today would put me further behind Marc and the rest of my fellow pilgrims, but I had no choice, I didn't want to make myself more ill.

Hontanas has a population of around seventy people and is so out of the way, it's only ever visited by pilgrims. Locals have to drive out of the town to get their post and other essentials, but there is a large church here that overshadows the rest of the tiny village. I met a man from Liverpool while I sat in the shade and he told me he was on his fourth Camino. He was probably in his late sixties and looked reasonably fit. We sat, talked and sipped some beers for a few hours, and he told me stories from his first Camino. I like hearing other people's stories from the Camino but I was feeling run down that day and I wasn't really taking it all in. I was just nodding my head politely, wishing my sunstroke would be gone by the morning. At around 4pm I decided to go and take a nap, as I truly was exhausted and hoping a sleep would make me feel better.

Four o'clock in the afternoon I fell asleep and I woke up at 4:30 the next morning. I'd slept for twelve and half hours! Apparently, the guy I'd met from Liverpool had tried waking me at 7pm for food, but I was out for the count. I woke up thinking I'd only been asleep a few hours, but it's fair to say I was feeling great. My sunstroke had vanished, I was no longer tired and could feel I was in for a good day of walking.

After dressing and sorting my bag out, I went and sat on a chair outside the albergue and planned how far I was going to walk that day.

While I was sitting there, around 5:15 a young girl who was working in the albergue came to me and handed me some fruit and bread, saying, 'I know you've slept a long time, so you must be hungry.'

I was very grateful and thanked her, offering her some money, but she refused to take it and wished me luck on the rest of the way. Another kind soul on the Camino. Looking at the guide today, apart from a steep climb early on, the rest of the walk was more of less flat. Today I was feeling the best I had since the start of the Camino and reckoned I could give it a real good go to get a lot closer to Marc and the gang.

As I was getting ready to leave, I saw the guy from Liverpool, and he was trying to make eye contact with me. I got the feeling he wanted to walk together, and I'm not a rude person by any stretch, but I smiled at him and got on my way. He would want to talk while walking and I felt that if I was on my own, I would cover more ground and would be able to think about the things back home that had led me to be on the Camino.

Hontanas – Fromista 34km

I decided I was going to aim for Fromista, 34km away.

That's hard going in this Meseta heat with no shade but since I'd left early and it's mostly flat, I decided to go for it. My guidebook told me that there isn't a water stop for the first 11km, so my water was full to the rim, with a back-up bottle in my backpack. First going off is quite difficult, with the steep incline, but I'd walked worse hills than this so far, so I pushed through.

Soon after, the incline becomes a straight path, and around 6km after setting off I arrived in a town called San Anton. There was a shop open here really early, but I had plenty of water so push on. Most shops on the Meseta are closed during the winter months, so if you walk the Camino during this time, please listen to the guidebook and take some water.

There are some beautiful ruins of a fourteenth-century monastery and the hospital of San Anton here. I could only imagine how beautiful the monastery must have been back then, because even in ruins, it's still beautiful. The route passes under a big Gothic arch and, according to the guidebook, in the fourteenth century, when the monastery had closed for the night, they would leave bread under this arch for the pilgrims who couldn't find anywhere to sleep or eat. The arch is now used for pilgrims to leave messages for loved ones who had passed. Apparently, the monastery was founded by a Frenchman in 1095, but the current building dates from the fourteenth century. The nineteenth letter of the Greek alphabet, 'Tau', was imprinted on the back of the habits that the monks wore, and the symbols can still be seen carved into the walls of the ruins, which was something I loved seeing.

After around a ten-minute stop here I kept walking. The sun was really beating down hard, and it was still early, but then again it was Spain, so what did I expect? I was just worried about the sunstroke coming back.

The path is flat and is basically just a dust road, so not a lot to write home about, but after an hour or so I came to a town called Castrojeriz. It's a fairly big town, so should have anything you need here. The town is over 2,000 years old, which is astonishing. As you walk into town, you see a statue of St James in pilgrim, so I took a selfie and kept walking.

I sat down at a tiny café and had some Spanish omelette with an orange juice and wrote a little in my diary, phoned home, smoked a cig and continued walking. I walk another 8.7km and arrived in Ermita de San Nicolás, where I was really surprised. For some reason I thought with a name like San Nicolás, the town would be big. But there wasn't even a town, it's literally just an albergue located close to the bridge over the river Pisuerga. The border between Burgos and Palencia is also here and apparently the albergue was built in the thirteenth century. It offered no electricity and was brightened by candlelight, keeping to the traditions of life on the Camino before modern invention. I will stay here the next time I walk the Camino Frances.

Only around 2.2km after leaving San Nicolás, you enter Itero de la Vega. Not much of anything here apart from another stunning statue of St James which I took another selfie with

before moving on. The next town was around 9km away and even though that doesn't sound a lot, it really was hot now. More dust roads and small numbers of people walking past me made me realise I'd only seen three or four pilgrims all day, and I began to wonder if a lot of pilgrims had chosen to skip this stage.

I got to the next town, which is Boadilla del Camino, and I was sweating from head to toe. I was now entering the region of Castile and León and there is a lovely Gothic church here. I looked at my map and my destination, Formista, was only 5.4km away, so I decided not to hang around. I'd made very good time so far today and really hoped I could catch up with Marc. I'd walked nearly 30km so far that day and I was feeling proud of myself, but I could tell I was starting to slow.

On the way to Formista, I was surprised by how many canals there are along this stretch. I later read that the canals were man-made during the 1800s to transport goods and are not used anymore, but they look beautiful as they take in the surroundings of the countryside. As you walk into Formista, you have to walk over a canal lock, which is pretty cool. Formista is one of the oldest towns on the Camino and was completely destroyed in the eighth century, only to be rebuilt in the tenth century.

I gathered I should find an albergue, get showered and change my clothes, ready to have a walk around town to see if I could find any of the group, as they should, by my calculation, be in Formista or else sadly just past it. I thought about texting Marc to see where he was, but I didn't want to as it's not the pilgrim way, even though I'd done it before. If you are meant to see people again, you will.

I stopped on the side of a road and began to get my guidebook out of my bag and what I heard next put a smile on my face. I didn't notice that where I'd stopped there was a path to my left leading to an albergue with tables and chairs outside. As I bent down to look for my map, I heard a voice yell 'Jorda-a-a-a-a-a-a-a-an.'

I looked around and couldn't have seen a better sight: Marc, Johan, Anna and Celine. I had a spring in my step again as I walked towards them to give them all a hug. They all had a bed but hurried me inside as they were running out quickly. Luckily enough I got one and had a shower after I'd unpacked.

As I walked outside into the albergue garden Marc handed me four cans of beer. He'd been to the shop while I was getting showered and thought he'd treat me. The group sat down to eat their salad while I placed my feet and the warm cans into a freezing cold bucket of water. Most of the pilgrims here were eating and the silence was beautiful as I sat and thought about how easy life is on the Camino and how addictive it was becoming. You just wake up every morning and walk, then do it all over again. If I could get paid and make a living out of walking the Camino I would do it for the rest of my life, no doubt about it.

As Johan had walked so far, I asked him what the most important thing he had learned about the Camino, and he told me this:

'I have learned to accept the kindness of others. If they offer me a beer, a small sweet or a steak meal, I say yes. For some people it's important for them to feel like they've done a good deed, so I accept and then return the favour to them.'

I loved that, and he was 100 percent right.

Celine and I got to know each other a lot more during the night as we both opened up to each other about our lives back home. She is such a sweet, caring girl but I felt that growing up wasn't particularly easy for her and it took her a while to trust someone enough to open up. She has a close bond with her mother though and they look after each other.

After the long chat with Celine and four beers later was around 19:30 and I was done for. It was a long walk today by my standards and I was very tried. I left the group still in the garden and headed off to bed, asking Marc to wake me in the morning so we could set off together.

Lying in bed, I remembered how relieved I was to not be on my own again and to have found my friends. We'd also heard that night that Skye was very far behind and suffering badly with her feet. Marc and I sadly wouldn't see Skye again, but we are all still in touch and all planning a Camino Reunion for 2021.

Fromista is world famous for its eleventh-century church and is considered the finest example of pure Romanesque in Spain. In medieval times Fromista was an important part of the Camino as it was home to many pilgrim hospitals. With a population of around 1,000, it is a fine example of a busy, yet tranquil town on the Camino.

'Jordan, wake up,' Marc whispered, nudging me awake. It was 5:15 and he'd decided we should start walking, which I was totally OK with. I'd had a good sleep and was feeling fighting fit. We looked in Marc's guidebook before we left and agreed the walk today would end in Carrión de los Condes, so if we lost each other while walking we could attempt to find each other.

Fromista – Carrión de los Condes 21km

The route today wasn't anything special, just a dusty path next to a dust road that had the odd tractor, but I enjoyed the peace. It wasn't long before Marc was in front of me and I was alone for most of the day's walk. When we left the albergue that morning Celine, Anna and Johan were still sleeping, so I didn't see anyone I knew, but it was a nice walk all the same. I didn't stop for around 14km that day and I believe my first stop was in a town called Villalcázar de Sirga, a town that was once a commandery for the Knights Templar. The church here is exquisite and has a shrine to the life of St James, paintings depicting his meeting with Jesus and his transference to Galicia.

It was still around 7km to Carrión de los Condes, so I decided to keep moving after my visit of the church was over. Carrión de los Condes has a population of around 3,000 and dates to around the year 800. It had a huge Jewish community back in 1290, with a population of around 11,000, but soon dwindled out, though the town's beautiful churches and monasteries remain. There are some great amenities here such as a bus stop, bank, souvenir shops, bars, restaurants and a Camino store to purchase backpacks and Camino t-shirts.

As I walked into town, I saw Marc leaning against a statue of St James. He was smiling at me and told me he'd found a private hotel room with three beds, for just ten euros each. He'd bumped into Mauricio while walking that day and he was already in the room showering. I was glad Mauricio was here; we hadn't seen him since Burgos, and it would be good to catch up.

The room was tiny and literally had just three beds inside and a tiny bathroom, but it was paradise compared to an albergue. I remember having a shower and taking a nap around 1pm, then waking up at 5pm to someone singing outside my hotel window. I'd only taken a nap and ended up sleeping for four hours and realised this was becoming a bit of a habit. The walking catches up on you sometimes; you think you're feeling good and ready to walk another ten miles, the next thing you're taking a four-hour nap. The sunstroke from the last couple of days wasn't helping either, though.

The song being sung outside my hotel window was *Ave Maria*, was my one of my granddad's favourite songs. It's also one of my favourite songs and when sung correctly it can be the most magical, powerful thing you will ever hear. The guy was probably in his mid-twenties and was playing an acoustic guitar while singing. I was standing there mesmerised by his voice and the way he was singing the song, watching him from the third-floor window. When he finished singing, I put on my trainers, went downstairs, walk outside and shook his hand. His version of that song is still the best I have ever heard, and I wish I'd recorded him.

I then decided to take a walk around town to see if I could bump into Marc and Mauricio and found them outside an ice cream shop eating frozen yoghurt. We all decided to go and get some proper food inside us and we found a restaurant close by. It was here I tried a food I'd always been curious about – *pulpo* (octopus). It came out on this huge plate with potatoes, lemon, garlic and French fries. Soon as I looked at it, I was instantly turned off by the look of the tentacles, but honestly, it is absolutely delicious. It kind of tasted like chicken but with more flavour and I ate *pulpo* any chance I got from that moment on. It's a delicacy in some of Spain's smaller towns and if you get a chance to try some, go for it. After food and another frozen yogurt, we decided to head back to the albergue and chill out for the night, sitting at a table inside playing cards, before hitting the sack around 9pm.

Just before bed, Marc delivered the bad news that Anna and Celine had taken a bus to Santiago and were flying home in a few days. This meant we wouldn't see Anna and Celine again, but like all my Camino family we regularly talk over the internet since arriving home. Celine has travelled to Australia and Japan in recent years and I hope she always sticks to travelling because she loves it.

I know this might sound strange, but since I was very young, I have had dreams where I am writing songs or poetry. In the dreams I'm always sitting at the same desk, one that I've never seen before, writing songs or poetry. I've never really understood it, but I wake up in the middle of the night, and I make sure I write them down. I've collected loads over the years and it still happens to me now. I'm not saying any of it is any good, but I know I couldn't do it while awake. That night in Carrión de los Condes, I wrote this poem in my dream:

> 'We walk, we walk
> we talk, we talk
> The days pass through
> Like I owe them to you
>
> How many more miles until a blister forms?
> Shall we sleep with the stars or in our dorms?
> Do we listen to the birds that sing every day
> Or listen to the pain that eats us away?
>
> If we keep on walking will we reach the end
> Or will we crawl on our knees around the very last bend?
>
> The heat is draining and the hills are steep
> But Santiago is calling and it's mine to keep.'

That's probably my favourite, out of the sixty-plus songs and poems I've written while sleeping. If any of you out there are sleep experts and can explain this to me, feel free to drop me a line. My email address is at the back of this book. I've always been curious to know why it only happens when I'm asleep.

Carrión de los Condes was taken from the Moors by Alonso Carreno around the year 800. In 1209, Hospital de la Herrada was established by a property tycoon who became steward of the king, to aid the pilgrims and other travellers.

Carrión de los Condes – Calzadilla de la Cueza 17km

A new day today and it was hard! Only a 17km walk but there was no shade whatsoever, along with no shops to refill water. We were planning on walking to Terradillos de Templarios but ended up stopping in Calzadilla de la Cueza. This is the proper Meseta now with 70 percent natural paths and the odd paved Roman road. Make sure you have plenty to eat and drink on this stretch as on the 17km from Carrión to Calzadilla, there is literally nothing at all.

After a while of walking alone I started chatting with a German girl called Ula. She seemed nice but kind of a closed book and wouldn't talk about Germany or her family back home, even though she had no problem asking me those kinds of questions. We basically walked the whole way together today and I found it quite hard to have a conversation with her without the conversation being brought back to German politics, and as you can imagine that's not really my strongest subject.

I was relieved after the 17km walk to see Marc, sitting on a bench outside an albergue in Calzadilla waiting for me. He wanted to continue walking, as Mauricio had continued, but when I noticed the albergue had a swimming pool and offered massage treatments from 5pm-8pm, I persuaded him to stay and enjoy what the place had to offer. Ula also decided she would stay with us and asked for a bed at the same time as Marc and me. Thankfully, she came out of her shell a bit during the rest of the day and wasn't so serious about everything.

After unpacking I shot outside to try out the pool and found it was so cold when I jumped in that I thought my heart was going to stop, but it was so refreshing at the same time. The albergue had a fridge behind the reception and was selling big bottles of beer for just two euros, so Ula and I took it in turns to buy the bottles and I think we had three each, while messing around with an inflatable ball in the pool. A couple of hours later we decided to visit the bar/restaurant down the street and grab a coffee, where we also had food, but I can't remember what we had.

After ordering and drinking her coffee, Ula told us she had no money on her as she hadn't seen a bank in a couple of days. That's totally normal on the Camino, but I told Marc ordering a coffee knowing full well you have no money is a bit cheeky. She knew one of us would have had to pay for it and I didn't like that, so I refused. Marc paid for her coffee and we headed back to the albergue where the massage therapist was setting her table up, and for me it was a glorious sight. Since the Camino began, I had been dying for a professional massage, as the weight of your backpack causes your shoulders to ache no end. I lay on her table for twenty-five minutes in total bliss while she got every knot out of my shoulders and back. I was like a new man walking in the morning and had none of the aches or pains I'd experienced for the last week. I think it cost me twenty euros for twenty-five minutes but believe me it was very much worth it.

After my massage Marc and I hopped into the hammocks outside in the garden and had a little nap. The place was so peaceful I could have slept for a week straight. On going to bed that night I got talking to a man from Belgium who was on his twelfth Camino. TWELFTH! He'd done different routes, like the Frances, Nord and Portuguese, but was on his twelfth Camino in total. Astonishing.

Calzadilla de la Cueza has a population of just sixty-eight people and dates back to the twelfth century.

Calzadilla de la Cueza – Sahagún 26km

Marc and I were up at 5:30 that morning and decided to start walking around 6:15, after Marc had finished his breakfast – the usual muesli. He lived on that stuff during the Camino. We decide to leave Ula in bed and start walking without her. She knew we were heading to Sahagún today, so she could catch up.

Not long into walking, Marc and I bumped into Johan and some of the new friends he'd met, one of them being James from Zimbabwe, a very nice man who was born in London and moved to the African continent when he was a child. He fought in the Zimbabwean Army and was witness to some very sad things during that time.

We all decided to walk together to Sahagún and my day consisted of walking with James and Johan, and listening to their life stories, which I loved it. Johan talked about his grandchildren and his long career as a lorry driver. He loved his grandkids to bits and missed them the most on the Camino and couldn't wait to be reunited with them when he eventually got back home.

The walk today was very pleasant, with no overly steep hills, and the bits of shade were very welcoming. We all arrived in a town called San Nicolás del Real Camino where some of us had breakfast and a drink in a little bar. We'd walked around 21km that day but being the Meseta there wasn't a great deal to talk about, as it was still flat with not a lot happening.

Arriving into Sahagún you are overwhelmed by all the ancient monuments on show. Sahagún was home to the famous Abbey of San Benito, which was founded in the tenth century and was to become one of the most important monasteries in Spain, but little is left of its remains. A lot of the ancient monuments here have been brought to their knees over time, mostly due to Arab invasions during the town's early years, but you can still see how beautiful they must have once been.

We all decided to head to the municipal for our night's rest and were greeted with a long line of pilgrims wanting beds, but twenty minutes later we were in and unpacking for the night. The sleeping area here was situated on the top floor of the municipal and had NO WINDOWS! To make it worse, the beds were made of plastic and your body just stuck to them, but when a bed costs six euros you deal with it.

After I'd had a shower, Marc and James were nowhere to be seen, so Johan and I sat down with some soup, bread and a few beers each. We sat there and talked for about five hours, drinking and getting to know each other better. We opened up to each other about some private things in our lives back home and became really good friends that night. I still talk to Johan daily and he has just completed his own book on the Camino called *Daar Gaat er Weer Een* (*There Goes Another One*).

After the day's sun and the afternoon's beer, I was ready to hit the hay by 7:30 and decided to go to bed. I didn't sleep at all again that night; it was too warm to put a cover over the plastic bed and too sticky to sleep on it without. Every two minutes I was tossing and turning, trying to get comfy, but nothing worked. Nearly everyone in the albergue was the same, so as people couldn't sleep, they began to talk. I put my headphones in and listened to some *Beautiful South* and some *Meat Loaf*. I ended up having around three hours' sleep.

As of 2018, Sahagún had a population of around 2,600. The first settlement of this site grew up around the nearby Benedictine monastery consecrated to the saints Facundus and Primitivus. The name Sahagún is thought to derive from an abbreviation and variation on the name San Fagun (Saint Facundus).

Sahagún – A barn in the middle of nowhere 27km

The next morning, we were walking to León, a real pinnacle place on the Camino for Marc and me, as we wanted to spend the night in the Parador Hotel. Martin Sheen stayed in this hotel in *The Way* and it looked amazing.

Marc had left before me that morning and was a fair bit in front of me, so I was playing catch up. The walk out of Sahagún is lovely as you pass over a historic, stone bridge that was built by the Romans in the eleventh century. After the bridge you continue on a glorious, but uneven Roman road that leads about 5km to a small town called Calzada de los Hermanillos. There is a little bar and restaurant at the start of town where I picked up some bread, cheese and a bottle of water and continued walking. I stopped for five minutes and wrote this in my diary:

'Today is one of the good days on The Way. The sun isn't too hot and I'm feeling I could walk forever and seems I didn't have much sleep, but I'm not tired at all. Marc is ahead of me today, but I don't mind as it's nice to walk alone as well as with company'.

Calzada De Los Hermanillos has a parish church, where there is a fantastic statue of St Bartholomew overpowering the Devil. I stared at it for a while, as I love statues like that, as they always give me a sense of the unknown. I'd walked just 13km and it was only 11am, so I decided I was really going to push it today and aim for a town called Reliegos. If I could reach it, I would have walked 30km, but the next part wasn't great.

When setting off from Calzada to Reliegos the heat hit 35 degrees and it was tough. There are no towns, no shade, no little shops and most importantly no water fountains, but that's the Meseta. The road you are walking on is classed as the most perfect stretch of Roman road left in Spain. Whatever time of year you walk this peaceful but nasty stretch, make sure your water bottles are full. This barren path is around 18km long and I started to feel the burning sun draining my body of energy around 5km into it. There is no albergue in between the towns, so I either had to turn back or fight through it. I decided to fight on.

Another hour passed. I'd walked 4km and the energetic pace I had that morning had become snail-like. That's the problem with me sometimes. I can't give up and make everything ten times harder for myself, but I believe what doesn't kill you makes you stronger. I looked at my guidebook and saw I had another 8 or 9km to go and just laughed to myself in disbelief, knowing I should have stayed in Calzada. I can usually do 5km in fifty minutes with no problem at all, but the next 5km took me just over two hours.

I noticed a farmer's barn just off the side of the path so I decided to have a rest and get my head down for a while on a bale of hay, hoping I would feel better after a nap. I woke up at 7pm to the noise of a tractor coming down the path, with the farmer signalling me to approach him, so I did. He told me I was one hour away from Reliegos and I'd probably missed my chance of a bed. I was angry with myself that I'd slept so long, yet I was hoping he'd soon go, so I could go back to sleep. It wouldn't have bothered me staying there all night; I needed the sleep and the peace. The farmer then kindly told me that if I wanted to use his barn for shelter until the morning, I could. I accepted and had the best night's sleep of my Camino. The night wasn't cold, and the hay was extremely comfortable. I absolutely loved it. I woke up around 3am and lay looking at the stars, peeking through the broken slats of wood, and felt an inner peace that I hadn't had in years. There is something magical about being alone and vulnerable during the night, especially when you have no clue where you are. At 4am I decided to get my torch out of my bag and do a bit of walking in the dark, which I absolutely loved. On my next Camino, I will definitely do a whole night of walking.

Reliegos was only 4km away from my location and if I got a move on, I might find Marc leaving the town for his day of walking. People later asked me how it had taken me so long and I took to the diary for my answer:

'People are asking me how it had taken me so long to walk the path today and why I ended up sleeping in a barn and not walking further. I feel some pilgrims find it a competition to see who can get to the next town the fastest, but I have absolutely no interest in that at all, that's not the pilgrim way. However long it takes you or however hard you find it, you do it your way and your way only. I'm not used to 35-degree heat, I'm not an experienced walker and I don't claim to be. If it takes me two days to walk 10km, nobody should care but me. It's my Camino'.

I told people this after a while of hearing 'How did it take you so long?' I'm not sure they liked my bluntness, but that's their problem, not mine. I texted Marc to let him know I was OK and that I was safe. He ended up walking past Reliegos and stayed in another town, but we decided to meet outside the Parador Hotel in León, 30km away.

A barn in the middle of nowhere – León 30km

So, at 4am I left the barn and got moving. After the day I'd yesterday it was good to hear from Marc and was I looking forward to seeing him. On leaving Reliegos you walk a rocky Roman road and pass many small towns over the next 10km or so. Mansilla de las Mulas Centro is the first town with an albergue. There is also a very large municipal that spreads across eight rooms and had eighty beds at five euros each. If you stay here, then please take a look around, as it's a lovely old town with a rich history. The name of the town is taken from *mano en silla* (hand on the saddle), which also describes the towns coat of arms. In medieval times it was a livestock market and has a beautiful wall surrounding the town that has been standing since the twelfth century.

According to my guidebook I was 20km from León and 'I'd enjoyed the walk so far. The weather was not too hot and there was a nice breeze in the air. Today was the first day I'd walked all day while listening to music. I kept my head down and just walked. You pass some towns such as Villarente, Arcahueja and Valdelafuente that all have albergues and cafés, so if you're tired you can stay somewhere before you get to León.

León. What a place.

As I entered this magnificent city full of architectural brilliance and busy streets, I decided to walk straight for the Parador Hotel and meet Marc without looking around first, as I'd missed my friend. Out of the many buildings on the Camino, the Parador Hotel in León took my breath away. It's not only enormous in length, but it's astonishing, Gothic look will leave you in awe. Outside the hotel is a statue of a pilgrim sitting down, looking to the skies, and Marc was sitting next to him like they were having a conversation. He got up when he saw me coming, rushed over and we gave each other a big hug. We talked for a few minutes and tried to decide where we were going to stay that night, and Marc suggested we actually stay in the Parador. We'd both wanted to stay there since seeing the hotel in the movie *The Way*, and we decided to go and enquire.

I asked the woman at reception if we could have the actual room that Emilio Estevez and Martin Sheen stayed in during filming and she told us we indeed could, for 168 euros.

Marc and I looked at each other for a few seconds, unsure about paying eighty-four euros each for one night. But when he smiled at me, I knew he wanted to stay, so I agreed, and we paid the money. This journey is once in a lifetime and we both ached all over and were due a bit of luxury. It's only money, right?

The room was superb, with a great shower and large balcony overlooking the square outside the hotel. Two single beds, TV, wi-fi and a mini-bar. I was in my oils. After around ninety minutes of us both showering and enjoying the room, we decided to go and explore the amazing city of León.

Marc and I were hungry and found a little pizzeria in the centre of town and both indulged in a margarita each. I remember it being something like eight euros for a 9-inch pizza, fries and a big beer. I don't turn down that type of offer. I was telling Marc just before we sat down to have dinner that I'd like a small tattoo of the Camino shell, to sit nicely with my religious tattoos, and he thought it was a great idea. While we were sitting there eating pizza, Marc took it as a sign that we happened to be sitting opposite a tattoo shop and nagged me to go and get it done. Forty minutes later and I was the owner of a new, small tattoo in the shape of a Camino shell. The guy who did the tattooing told me that the pilgrims wanting Camino tattoos were his biggest clientele and he'd got a good little business there. Marc was out with his camera and found it hilarious that part of it hurt and basked in my pain.

After my arm was strapped up, we headed out to the main square of León and sat in front of its magnificent cathedral with a coffee. Sitting there I met another person from Wales, but I can't remember what part he was from. He was cycling the Camino with his wife and wore a t-shirt with the Welsh flag sprawled across it. I stopped him and asked him for a picture, before he was back on his bike and on with his journey. León was extremely busy and there were queues in every bar, café and shop, so we decided to go back to the hotel and make the most of what we'd paid for. The hotel really is stunning. Even if you're not staying there, poke your head in and have a look. It was quite funny that even though Marc and I separated our single beds in the hotel room, there was a border going around the room with love hearts on that Marc and I hadn't noticed. When he sent his wife Irma a photo of our room, she noticed the love hearts and told him we looked cute, so we pulled our beds even further apart.

Breakfast was included with the price of our hotel room (should think so, as well) and was served between 6am and 8:30. Marc and I were the first ones down in the breakfast hall as we wanted to have an early start walking. Today would be one of our longest days on the Camino, with us walking 36km to Hospital de Órbigo.

With a population of around 135,000 plus the tourists and pilgrims, you can imagine that León is a busy place, busting with shops, transport links and restaurants. León was once a Roman military base, hence the name León, taken from the word legion. The year 910 saw the beginning of one of its most prominent historical periods, when it became the capital of the Kingdom of León which took part in the Reconquista against the Moors. In 1188, the city hosted the first Parliament in European history while under the reign of Alfonso IX, and is home to its historic, Gothic cathedral. It was founded in the first century and you can't even begin to imagine the history of the place, most of which we probably know nothing about.

León – Hospital Del Órbigo 36km

The breakfast here was something else. Marc and I still talk about this breakfast and say it was the best we had all walk. Proper cooked breakfast with sausages, bacon, eggs, fried bread, beans, hash browns and mushrooms. Then you had the cereal and fruit counters that Marc and I took advantage of to stock up on some apples and bananas for the walk ahead.

Marc and I were out of the hotel door by 7am. It didn't take Marc long to get ahead of me and I ended up walking alone again for the whole of the day, but it came as a blessing and was the single most important day of walking I had on the Camino. Everyone that had walked the Camino before me always said the same things on their blogs/videos: 'There will come a day of reflection on the Camino that you cannot get away from,' and they were right. Today was the day of reflection for me and the day I finally let go of the things back home that were weighing me down.

I also read countless times on different forums and blogs that at some point on the Meseta would come the moment of your Camino that really tests your metal strength, as you are left alone with your thoughts, and for some people that can be a challenging thing. Today was the first time I realised I was on the Camino and had travelled so much in the last few years because I was running away. Not running away in the sense of leaving home and never coming back but running away from myself and the wrong decisions I had made in life. It seemed that travelling was the only thing that made me forget everything, and it's a strange thing, because at the time you don't realise that you're running from anything. You only realise when you're there.

When I was twenty-one, I worked abroad as holiday rep in Menorca. I absolutely loved the job, and I did a bit of singing, dancing and children's entertainment. About six months into the job I fell totally in love with a girl from Huddersfield, West Yorkshire. She was beautiful, kind, funny and we were totally infatuated with each other. After her two-week holiday was over, I knew I couldn't let her go back to the UK without me; nothing else mattered apart from being with her. I quit my job, went home to Wales to pack more clothes and moved to Huddersfield to be with her. Quick, but when you know – you know. I ended up staying there three years, but in the end the break-up was horrible and totally my fault. I missed home, my family, my friends and I wasn't very nice to her because of it. I struggled to find full-time jobs, pay rent, do nice things with her, and it made me miserable. I don't think she realised how much it used to bother me and I should have spoken to her more. She never made me miserable, though, the situation did, and the break-up wasn't her fault one bit. But strangely, I resented her every single day from the moment we broke up, to this exact day on the Camino. Why? I don't know, as she did absolutely nothing wrong. From the break-up to the Camino, three years had passed, and I still wasn't over it. I couldn't admit to myself that

I had messed up and lost one of the best things I had in my life. I could have gone home and visited my family and friends anytime I wanted and could always have gone back to her, even though I couldn't always afford to, but the idiot inside me ended up losing her for good. I think when you make a mistake that you can't rectify, you begin to hate yourself for it, and that's a horrible feeling. I hated the thought of her being with someone else because of the mistakes I made and that's what I was always running from. I ran from that for three years. Travelling and drinking myself into oblivion most days were the only thing that helped me escape from it, but even after three years she was still on my mind every day. I knew I was on the Camino to get away from those thoughts and feelings, but I couldn't admit to myself that I was the one to blame. Walking alone with those thoughts inside my head changed me a lot. I didn't come on the Camino looking for answers but being alone with just your thoughts and no distractions, you find your answers. It dawned on me that day that I didn't hate her for leaving me, I hated myself for causing it to happen. I didn't hate her for being with someone else, I hated myself for being lonely. It's a hard thing to have to admit to yourself, but there comes a point when you have to, and I couldn't go another three years pining over the same woman who had now moved on. It would have ended up killing me. It was only now when I looked back on those three years after the break-up, I realised how depressed I was. I hit the drink pretty hard and would go out almost every night by myself and drink myself into oblivion to try and forget about it. When something bad happens to me, I tend to turn to a bottle, and I know that's something I must keep control of in life. I live in a poor community where a lot of people end up alcoholics, and I've lost count of the amount of people I've known die from it over the years. I never want to end up down that road; I know first-hand how easily it can happen. The break-up really did affect me and that's the reason I have stayed single for eight years after the breakup, because I can't go through something like that again. Truthfully, even after nearly nine years apart I don't think I'm 100 percent over what happened.

It all become too much that day, and it hit me as I sat with my back to a tree and cried my eyes out for twenty minutes. I hadn't done that since the day we broke up. I cried because I missed her, cried because I missed her family who treated me like one of their own and I cried because I felt guilty for hurting her. I often think about arguments we had when we were together, arguments that I always started. I get angry with myself that I was so mean with my words and would give anything to tell her how sorry I am for being that way towards her, but she doesn't want anything to do with me and I fully understand that. I'm not the same person anymore and when I think back, I hate the person I was when I was with her. The stress of living there and struggling to make ends meet every day made me a horrible person but letting it all out and giving myself a few home truths was what I needed. I just wish I had done it years ago. I still think of her a lot; I'm bound too as she was a big part of my life. I hope she's happy and living a great life, whatever she's doing. We haven't spoken in nearly nine years now, but I like to think that one day we could be friends again. I hope her family are well and believe me when I say this, her family are absolute diamonds. We live 300 miles apart, so it's not like I can just go and see how they are all doing, but I hope they are all happy.

Being alone with just your thoughts on the Camino can be the most terrifying, soul-destroying, but equally most important thing that can happen to you. That day changed my life, no doubt about it. I realised what was wrong with my personality and what I needed to change about myself. I have the Camino to thank for that.

While walking that day I passed through a town called Puente de Órbigo which has one of the longest medieval bridges in Spain and dates from the thirteenth century. The bridge would host jousting tournaments during the 1400s and witnessed a battle when the Visigoths slaughtered the Swabians here.

As I entered Hospital de Órbigo, I noticed an albergue with its doors wide open and a few pilgrims all laughing and joking in the doorway. Marc was one of them.

'Jordan, I've reserved us both a bed,' he called out to me. 'We will stay here for the night.'

It was a lovely little place called Albergue San Miguel, and paintings filled every wall. The paintings were made by pilgrims who stay in the albergue and there were hundreds spread around. After I paid my seven euros for the bed and had showered, I sat down at the paint board and began my masterpiece. To be fair it was a pretty terrible painting, but the albergue's owner found a place for it on his wall. I hope it's still there the next time I walk the Camino. It would be nice to see it again and imagine the thousands of pilgrims that must have looked and laughed at it. While I was channelling my inner Picasso, Marc had a look around the small town and was back by the time I'd finished. We decided to have some food and sit outside, where we met a Spaniard named Juan Carlos. Juan's English wasn't brilliant, but between his broken English and my little Spanish, we communicated just fine. We sat talking about football for about three hours and I really enjoyed it. He was a massive Barcelona fan and really knew his stuff about them. I had a brilliant night's sleep that night in a very comfortable bed and didn't want to get up in the morning. I can't remember what time I went to bed, but I know it was early. I was still a bit mentally drained after the day and wanted to get my head down. The next day we were walking to Astorga, another hard but eye-opening walk.

Hospital de Órbigo was a battle site in 456 between forces loyal to Theuderic I and Rechiar. The long, stone medieval bridge here would hold jousting tournaments during the 1400s and was once demolished by the town's inhabitants, to slow the advance of Napoleon's forces into Spain. As of 2018, there was a population of around 1,000 here.

Hospital de Órbigo – Astorga 17km

We only walked around 17km today, but it was a splendid walk. After a hard walk uphill, we came to La Casa de los Dioses, where a man named David had been living on the mountain for the last five years. He lived in a self-made hut and offered free fruit and water to passing pilgrims, though most pilgrims give a donation. He greeted every pilgrim with a hug and told Marc and me that he loved the freedom of living on the mountain, and meeting so many pilgrims was a blessing. Fair play to the man, he's giving his life to the Camino. I later read online that he left the mountain a couple of years after we met him but missed it so much, he returned and is now living there again, where he is somewhat of a celebrity on the Camino.

We passed a little town called Villares De Órbigo that has a parish church dedicated to St James, and a short while later passed through

Cruceiro de Santo Toribio. Santo Toribio has a stone cross commemorating the fifth century Bishop Toribio of Astorga, who was apparently banished from the town and is credited with having brought a relic of the cross from Jerusalem.

The walk was filled with hills today and I was relieved as we finally arrived into Astorga, after seeing the busy town in the distance for most of the day's walk. We booked into the municipal and explored a little, as Astorga is a lively town with plenty of bars, restaurants, shops and banks. I had a pain in one of my calves from walking and, after some pasta and a beer, decided to have a lie down in the municipal. Around six o'clock in the evening, while I was lying on my bed texting my loved ones back home, I started talking to a girl called Bea, who told me that there was a group of pilgrims having a drink at the bar up the road and I should join them. I'm not one to say no to a beer, so I agreed, and was delighted to see Juan Carlos was with the group, who were all enjoying jugs of sangria. Juan was sitting with Erin Elizabeth and Marcy Landes, both from the United States. Marcy had an incredible singing voice and Erin's uncle was a famous astronaut, though I can't remember his name.

We sat drinking and getting to know each other over the next few hours and when the bar closed, we sat outside the albergue and continued with our love for sangria. Erin and Marcy soon went to bed, leaving me and Bea outside to drink and talk. Bea was such a funny girl and she had the best jokes. Even on the hardest days of walking, with every part of your body wanting to give up, she would come out with a one-liner that would buckle you with laughter, and I love people like that. When I woke up the next morning everyone had gone. I looked across the room and saw that it was just me and Bea remaining, the two people with the hangover from hell. I woke her up and told her that the group had gone, and after around thirty minutes we left together. Today was going to be very, very tough for Bea and me.

Astorga has a population of around 11,000 and was founded in 14 BC by Emperor Octavian, who originally named it Asturica Augusta. Because of its location, Astorga was a place for pilgrims to rest and get ready to climb the forthcoming mountains. Astorga once had twenty-one hospices. Today, there is the Hospital de las Hermanas de la Caridad, which is a medical facility in front of the cathedral.

Astorga – Foncebadón
27km

It wasn't so much the hangover because that disappeared after a couple of hours. Today's trek was uphill all day, in scorching heat, and it sucked the life out of us. We were literally crawling in some parts; it was so hot. We stopped and had a rest every ten minutes or so, and what should have taken us around five hours to get to Foncebadón took us eight hours. As we left around 7am, we got into the albergue at 3pm, but still early enough to enjoy the afternoon.

As we got to the top of the last hill, we saw an albergue in the distance with a balcony spreading across the back wall. Marc, Erin, Juan Carlos and Marcy were all waving to us, congratulating us on finally getting there. Bea and I had never been so happy to see an albergue in our lives. Foncebadón is situated on a mountain, is very secluded, and signals the end of the Meseta. I was relieved the Meseta was over with, but I will always look back on it as the place in Spain that changed me as a person. A magnificent, horrifying, boiling, eye-opening stretch of land that forces you to find yourself.

Thanks to the Camino, the once abandoned town of Foncebadón is stirring back to life. We joined the others, and all had a bed in the same dorm. There was only one other person in the dorm with us, a French guy who we nicknamed 'Horse' after Bea walked in on him having a shower.

It was here Marc and I found our favourite restaurant on the Camino, the only restaurant in the town. It was a medieval-themed restaurant, with the waiters and waitresses dressed up in medieval clothes for added effect. The menu only had two items on it, a medieval steak or a medieval burger. But that's all it needed, as it was the best food I have had in the whole of Spain. There wasn't one piece of porcelain in the whole building, as meals were served on a plate of flat bread, while your water was served in a wooden beaker. They nailed the medieval theme down to the last thought, it was brilliant. The owner came to talk to us and told us that the meat was farmed locally. He wasn't joking, as next to the restaurant was a field full of cows that belonged to them. We all sat, along with our new friend Horse, and had a great evening of food and laughter. Later we all sat on the balcony and all drank water. After the night before I don't think any of us could handle anything alcoholic. The balcony had a mesmerising view of the mountain's way back in the distance – the ones we'd slowly passed over in the last couple of weeks. I could have sat there for days, but we all hit the sack at around 8pm, because for Marc and me, tomorrow would be an important day. We'd both been waiting for this day for a long, long time.

Foncebadón flourished during the Middle Ages, offering shelter and hospitality to the pilgrims who passed through on their way to Santiago. According to local tradition, the village was granted a tax exemption in return for planting 800 stakes in the ground to mark the path leading to the village. In the tenth century, Ramon II of León convened a religious council in the village and in the eleventh or twelfth century, the hermit Gaucelmo established a hospital and a church.

Foncebadón – Ponferrada 27km

Walking to Ponferrada today, we passed Cruz de Ferro. It stands 5,000 feet above sea level and the lonely iron cross atop an aging, wooden pole meets the many pilgrims that come to see it. Over the many years it has become one of the abiding symbols of the Camino and is, especially for Marc, a life-changing moment for many. By tradition, a pilgrim will collect a stone from their hometown and carry it across the Camino until they lay it down at the foot of this cross. This stone symbolises your problems, fears or regrets, and by laying the stone down at the foot of the cross, you are leaving your problems behind.

Marc had brought three stones with him.

- One for his family, to keep them safe.
- One for his mother.
- One he collected on the Camino for Fritz, to bring his wife some much-needed good luck.

I can't really put into words what happened for Marc at Cruz de Ferro, so it's best to hear it from him.

Marc:

'One of the reasons I was walking the Camino is because I carry a burden. My mother died seven years ago of a blood clot and was in a coma for three days, in which time I never left her bedside. I never really recovered from her death and the stone I placed for her at Cruz de Ferro was me finally saying goodbye to her. When my father heard I was walking the Camino he wished me good luck with a smile and now I know why. After a week of walking, I recognised that I didn't get tired at all. Most pilgrims would be sleeping, and I could have easily kept on walking, so I would go and explore the towns. When I called my father and told him that I was never tired, he told me that it was because my mother was with me, carrying me. He also told me that before she died, he asked his wife to look after me on my travels. From that day I felt like I was cheating on the Camino as I had my mother carrying me, which was the reason I was never tired. But hearing that from my father also gave me strength for the rest of the Camino.

The next morning around 6:30, when Jordan and I left the albergue, there was a thick fog that had set in overnight. Normally I would be sad about this as I wanted to be at Cruz de Ferro with sunshine, but everything happens for a reason, I thought, and we walked together in the fog. We saw the cross in the distance, and I felt this energy come over me that made me want to run. I needed to get to the cross as quickly as I could, and I apologised to Jordan and started running. I don't know why, but I had a feeling that my mother was there waiting for me. From the very beginning of the Camino I believed she would be there, waiting for me, and she was. As I got to the cross, I felt a warmth and energy in the surroundings that I had never felt before. I laid down the first stone for Anita, the wife of Fritz, and hoped she had a speedy recovery from her illness. The second stone I left for my family and asked that they are always kept safe. It was still extremely foggy as I took a selfie with the cross behind me. While taking the selfie, I laid the stone for my mother at the foot of the cross and thanked her for helping me and always being with me. That exact second a blue sky broke open, with a beautiful sunrise, and shone onto Cruz de Ferro. I took the picture and again thanked my mother. As I turned to look at the sunrise, the fog quickly set back in, covering the sun and the blue skies. All within a few seconds the fog broke, the sun came out, and then the fog set back in again. The sun appeared the exact moment I thanked her and placed the stone.

She came to say hello and she was with me. I know it.'

Marc hugged me and cried for a few minutes. Not tears of sadness, but happy tears of knowing she was with him. I stood there, a few yards away from him, and saw myself the change in the weather at that moment. It was eerie and I also believe it was his mother. She wanted him to know she was there.

The fog stayed until nightfall and the only sun we had that day was the few seconds while he placed the stone.

Cruz de Ferro had a different effect on me, and I felt like this was the end of my Camino and I didn't want to continue anymore. If there was an airport around the corner, I think I'd have flown home that day. I placed down one rock at the cross on which I'd written 'I'm sorry'. The reason I wrote that will stay between Marc and me. I kissed the rock, placed it down, and at that moment I felt like that was what all this had been about, saying sorry. I felt like a new person and didn't have anything to be sorry for anymore. I realised that was why I was on the Camino, to make amends in my own way. I've never been a bad person, not really. Got into stupid, drunken fights more than I should have, said some horrible things to the people I love, been in trouble with the police a few times. But I'm not a bad person, I just make stupid decisions sometimes, as we all do. Marc always calls me a lovable rogue, a tough shell with a big heart, and he's right. But I felt it was now over with and I'd gained a clean slate. Marc and I sat on a bench looking at the cross and cried together for about ten minutes. Cruz de Ferro had touched us both in different ways but had brought us even closer together. That memory will stay with me forever and I told Marc that I thought my journey to Santiago had come to an end. He didn't want me to go home and told me that if this was the end for me then so be it, but I should just enjoy the rest of the Camino to Santiago, and then at least I could say I completed the whole pilgrimage. He was right, and even though it felt like the end for me it wasn't, but I wouldn't realise that until I got to Santiago.

After leaving Cruz de Ferro we soon caught up with Erin and Marcy, who had stopped and were having a coffee in a town called Acebo. We didn't tell them what had happened at the cross, as it was mine and Marc's moment and we wanted to keep it that way. Actually, writing about it in this book is the first time I've ever spoken about it.

We continued walking and entered a beautiful town called Molinaseca Puente de los Peregrinos via a handsome medieval bridge leading to a seventeenth century church called San Nicolás. On passing the church I happened to see an old, worn painting nailed to the door of a house that was sheltered by a large balcony. The painting was of a pilgrim walking towards Santiago Cathedral with the sunrise in the distance. Looking at the bottom corner of the painting I noticed the date was 21/11/1925, the exact date my beloved nan was born. I was meant to see that painting and believed that was a sign, telling me that I had to continue to Santiago. 'Message received,' I said to myself and off I went. Marc actually turned around at that point and took a picture of me looking at the painting and it's one of my favourite photos from my Camino.

The rest of the walk was mostly downhill, and I lost pace with the others before seeing them in a town called Ponferrada, where they were waiting outside an albergue. This was another donation albergue, so Marc and I gave our usual five euros and got showered. There was a massive garden here and plenty of taps and washing lines for us to do some laundry, so we did just that. Afterwards we headed to the supermarket for some food as we were going to cook tonight.

I told Marc I hoped Mauricio was OK as we hadn't seen him for a few days. Then, as we turned the corner, he was walking towards us with a woman. We then realised why we hadn't seen him for a few days. He's a typical Italian, is Mauricio, and he loves the ladies. Since the Camino he's moved to Ukraine, where I've been to visit him, and he's the same there, the women love him. The woman he was walking with was called Janet and was from California, I think. She reminded me of an American reality TV star with blonde hair, fake boobs, Botox and lip-filler. She was a lovely, quiet lady who was good company for us all, and it was also great to see our Italian friend again.

Marc, Mauricio, Marcy, Erin, Janet, Juan Carlos and I all congregated in the albergue's kitchen and made a salad. I absolutely hate salad. I got to know Erin and Marcy a lot better that night and they are wonderful girls. They didn't come on the Camino together, though; they actually met in

Barcelona a few weeks before while enjoying a gap year, and both decided to leave their job and do the Camino. Marcy is an open book and talks freely about herself, but Erin, on the other hand, is a bit more reserved. I got the feeling that maybe things weren't great back home and that's why she was travelling. As we were all sitting there talking and laughing, I was wishing Michele was with us. It had been so long since I'd seen her, and while the rest of my favourite pilgrims were with me, she was missing. I hoped I would see her again, while also hoping she was safe. Not long later I decided to sleep and put an end to a very emotional few days.

Ponferrada is a modern metropolis with a population of around 65,000. Most of the sights here are in the centre of the medieval city and the Camino path takes you next to them all. There is an iron bridge called 'Pons Ferrata', where the city gets its name, and it's built on the back of a coal-mining reserve that has been used since the medieval times.

Ponferrada – Villafranca del Bierzo 25km

Marc and I woke up early today. Everyone else was sleeping, so we decided to get going, knowing they'd catch up. Ponferrada is quiet and not many pilgrims were around as we left. We were heading for Villafranca del Bierzo around 25km away, and as I always struggled with the heat on the Camino, today was amazing, as we had rain. It was the first rain of the whole Camino and I absolutely loved it. While the Spanish pilgrims were putting on their raincoats, I was taking layers off and walking in a thin t-shirt and shorts. My walking also improved, as no heat meant I was walking like a bullet, and Marc and I were really moving. That 25km walk was done in four hours. I enjoyed it more when it was just me and Marc walking together. When I was feeling good, I could match his pace, and we got some serious walking done together.

We passed one of the most amazing castles I'd ever seen that day, a magnificent twelfth century templar castle. It's recently been declared a national monument and has reopened its doors to the public.

Fuente Cacabelos was the next major village we passed through, which once homed five medieval pilgrim hospices. There are plenty of hotels and albergues here if you wish to stay, but Marc and I walked straight through. As we entered Villafranca, we noticed a hotel advertising private rooms, so we enquired about the price. The man in reception told us that he could offer a private room with two single beds for thirty euros and we snapped his hand off. Fifteen euros each for a night of no snoring and rustling backpacks at 5am would do us both great.

It had rained all day and it continued to rain throughout the night as we went out for dinner, where we bumped into Juan Carlos, Erin and Marcy. They were eating pizza, so we joined them for a slice. They were also sitting with two sisters from the Basque country who were both studying to be doctors. We would only meet them for this one night, but they were lovely girls and great company.

Villafranca isn't a big place, but it's full to the brim with bars, restaurants and Camino gift shops. The rain was really hammering down, and most bars were closing, so Marc and I decided to go back to the hotel for a game of chess.

The thing that struck me about this idyllic town was that for a population of just 5,000, it has seven different churches and monasteries, and that seemed a lot. The first human settlements in the area date to the Neolithic age, while the first historically known people living here were the Celtiberians. The Spanish general Antonio Filangieri died here.

Villafranca – Las Herrerias 23km

The next morning the rain had gone, and the sun was back, much to Marc's delight. Today could be split into two paths: a steep walk over the mountains or a gentle climb through the many villages and highways on the way to Las Herrerias. Marc decided he wanted to take the mountain route, and I decided I'd like to walk alone on the much easier path. Again, I enjoyed my time alone and the peacefulness it brought. I thought a lot about my family that day and realised that I'd been so caught up in the Camino, I hadn't spoken to them in a while, so I stopped at several different bars along the way and checked in with them all. My grandmother was ninety years old when I was on the Camino and her memory wasn't what it was. When I phoned her, she asked if I was in work, and when I was coming to visit her, so I had to explain to her that I was walking across Spain and I wouldn't be home for a little while. After ending the conversation, I felt sad that her memory was leaving her, and she couldn't remember relatively easy things. It made me realise how lucky I was to be young, healthy and able to travel. I missed her dearly on the Camino and phoned her more often for the rest of the journey. She has sadly died since, and I miss her more than anything.

Around 20km into it, I was walking into a town called Vega de Valcarce, where I saw Marc standing in a coffee shop doorway, taking photographs of the mountains he'd just walked across. It had taken us the same amount of time to reach Valcarce and we laughed at how we always ended up finding each other. We'd only walked around 5km more when we entered a tiny village called Los Herrerias and, to my delight, saw someone I hadn't seen since my very first day on the Pyrenees.

Sitting outside an albergue/bar was Tiffany, the good-looking American girl who'd offered to help me on the Pyrenees when she thought I was dying. We hadn't seen each other since that day, and it was lovely to see her again, so I thanked her for looking out for me up on the mountain and she laughed.

She was sitting with another person I'd also said hello to on the first day, a girl named Beth Cox from Gloucestershire. With them were two men from Ireland, James and Noel. Out of that group, I regularly speak to Beth on social media. She was working for the BBC at the time of the Camino but is now a digital communicator for the police in Gloucester, near Bristol. A very smart, pretty girl with an incredible singing voice, and she's also part of a band now.

They'd all booked a room in this albergue, so Marc and I decided to stay there too. Tiffany told us that in the morning we had to walk 10km uphill and it wasn't going to be easy. I looked in my guidebook and she was right, but they had a plan. The man living next door to the albergue had his own business that allowed you to rent one of his horses and ride the entirety of the 10km climb. I didn't like the idea at first and felt I should walk, but then remembered that ancient pilgrims would travel the Camino on horseback, and it's not actually cheating at all. Marc decided he wanted to walk, so Tiffany, Beth, Noel, James and I decided to pay the man for his services and agreed to meet him at 7am in the morning outside the albergue.

The albergue was lovely. They had a sheepdog that I spent a good hour playing fetch with outside, until Tiffany and I decided to sit down with a pack of cards while the others went to eat. Every time Tiffany and I spoke we seemed to flirt with each other. It wasn't intentional, but it was obvious we fancied each other and was obvious from the first time we spoke up on the mountain, so I let her win at cards, obviously. We all met after dinner and enjoyed a few beers in the bar up the road. Seems I wasn't walking first thing in the morning. I ended up having more than a few and can't remember getting to bed… again.

Las Herrerias is a town I don't know much about. It's very small, and I'd guess at the population being around ten. I've tried to research any historical events that happened here, but I drew a blank.

Las Herrerias – Triacastela 30km

The morning arrived and the five of us were ready to get on our horses and enjoy the easy ride to O Cebreiro, where we would then walk to Triacastela. We passed many little towns on the way up and had to stop our horses many times for passing tractors and pilgrims. The owner of the horses walked in front of us all leading the way, choosing not to go on horseback. I kept myself amused by making my horse run a few times, which made the horses behind run with it, to the horror of the girls, who were scared out of their minds when their horses suddenly started sprinting. This led me to be called a few names that I can't repeat in this book.

After two hours we reached the top and we were all aching. Our legs and backs were in pieces from sitting on the horses and I hadn't realised that would happen.

When we started walking again, we passed O Cebreiro Iglesia, the oldest surviving building on the Camino and the oldest surviving church in the whole of Spain. Built in the ninth century, it's astonishing to imagine how many pilgrims have entered its forever aging doors. The church is also the resting place of Don Elías Valiña Sampedro, the parish priest who dedicated his life to restoring and preserving this route of the Camino. It was his idea to mark the Camino with the yellow arrows we'd all followed endlessly for over a month, and there is a bust of his head that overlooks the church, which many pilgrims touch as a token of good luck. He died in 1989 and will forever be known as an integral part of how we walk the Camino today.

It was here that we now entered Galicia, which many people believe to be the final stretch to Santiago, now only eight days away. O Cebreiro to Triacastela is around 20km and all downhill, so we got moving.

In a place called Fonfría we saw Marc. He'd left a good while before us and was rightly in front when we saw him sitting outside a little bar. Triacastela was around 10km away now and Tiffany and I spend the whole way walking together, while Marc was in front with the rest of the group. Even though it was downhill and an easy walk, I knew I was starting to feel the strain of walking every day again. I'd need a rest day soon to recharge my batteries.

We all shared a dorm in Triacastela and were joined by someone the girls had met along the way. His name was Mark Sutherland and was a great bloke who, again, I still talk to on social media. We all went for a meal in a restaurant with a pilgrims' menu for ten euros. While there, Tiffany's and my flirting began really taking off, and I could sense something was going to happen between us soon.

I told the group I'd felt a little faded over the last few days and I thought it was time I had a rest day. I hadn't had one since Pamplona. When we got back to the albergue we all sat drinking some local wine for a few hours and people started leaving the table to go to bed. At the end of the night it was only Tiffany and I still awake, and when the last glass was empty, we shared a kiss before going to bed.

I woke up with the other pilgrims the next morning and, even though I wanted to walk, I was still so faded, I needed a break, just a full day to recharge my batteries. I told Marc I would catch up with him in the next couple of days and I booked into the hotel across the road. I thought everyone had gone, but I got a text message from Tiffany saying she'd also decided to have a rest day, so I snuck her into my hotel room to save her paying for another room. She showered and we decided to go for some breakfast and a walk next to the river just out of village.

At around midday we got back to the hotel room and stayed in bed together until the next morning. Again, I didn't come on the Camino for anything like this and I certainly didn't expect it to happen once, never mind twice. I still missed Kim and wished she hadn't taken the bus ahead of us, but as far as I was concerned, I was never to see her again. Tiffany really was my type of woman, though, and there was no way I was saying no to her. My rest day wasn't so relaxing after all, but you're only young once, right?

Triacastela gets its name from the three castles that once stood here, none of which exist today. Norman invaders in 968 AD pillaged here, eventually to be defeated at Cebreiro pass and driven away from town. It is thought they destroyed the castles at this time. It has a population of around 700.

Triacastela – Sarria
19km

At 7am the next morning, Tiff decided she was going to take the bus forward a few towns to meet her friend Nicole, who she'd come on the Camino with. I didn't want to take a bus and decided I'd walk the 20km to Sarria, where Marc and I had arranged to meet. I hadn't realised that there was, again, two paths you could take today, and Marc and I would separately take different paths.

I came to a town called Samos, which has an enormous monastery and a silent river running next to a coffee bar, where I decided to stop. Samos has a few albergues and hotels you can use, if you want to stay in this peaceful, postcard town. Just after leaving Samos I got a phone call from my mother explaining that a friend of mine back home had sadly, suddenly died. I was in a bit of shock and don't really remember the next stretch of the walk to Sarria very much. On arriving in Sarria, though, I was taken aback by how busy it was. The municipal there had a line leading right around the large, square building. Every restaurant, bar and souvenir shop was full. It's an absolute nightmare after a long walk, as you just want your bed and a shower.

I finally met up with Marc and we got a table outside a bar, where there were a couple of American men sitting. Marc told me that Sarria is the starting place for thousands of people walking the Camino every year. Sarria to Santiago is 100km and is the minimum distance you can walk on the Camino to be eligible for your Compostela.

Marc rang around a few local hostels, albergues and hotels before finally getting us a private room in a hostel. Marc and I didn't like Sarria at all; a lovely place but way too crowded for us. This might be an unpopular thought, but surely pilgrims who have walked from Saint-Jean-Pied-de-Port in France, gotten their passports stamped in countless towns and are extremely tired – surely they should have the first beds in the municipals? But for the people who own the albergues, it's all about the money to them and they don't think like pilgrims, unless they've walked the Camino themselves.

After showering, Marc and I walked around town looking for a restaurant with space available and bumped into Tiffany and Nicole. She'd only taken the bus a short distance to catch up with her friend. We all found space to eat and were joined by Mauricio after a little while. What was becoming a bit of routine when Mauricio and I were together at night, we again got blind drunk and laughed long into the night. At least I remember getting to bed that night, that doesn't usually happen.

Sarria has a population of around 12,000 people and, with its Celtic origins, was once a major medieval centre for pilgrims with many churches, chapels, monasteries and several pilgrim hospitals.

Sarria – Portomarín
25km

On leaving Sarria it was busy, with what seemed like thousands of school children on their summer holidays walking the last 100km with their teachers. New pilgrims in their clean clothes, perfect boots and with high energy levels. Marc told me Sarria and the number of people starting here had made him feel more like a tourist than a pilgrim, so we decided to go for it today and get as far in front as we could. I have no bad feelings about people starting in Sarria and I hope they enjoyed their Camino; it was just too busy for us. We were just used to seeing a few pilgrims every day and walking in peace.

We bumped into Erin, Marcy and Juan Carlos while starting out and it was great to see them again. We walked together for a few minutes, but Marc and I were a lot quicker and lost them just outside a town called Barbadelo. After around an hour we seemed to have got away from the bustling crowds and we stopped at a café in Morgade for an orange juice and coffee. We were in rural Galicia now and were steadily climbing, knowing we would soon be crossing the Galician mountains.

A while later we passed a town called Mercadoiro which has the unusual statistic of being a town with a population of ONE, as the same person owns the albergue and adjoining café. We were only 6km away from Portomarín and as that was our destination for the day, Marc decided to have a coffee while I played with a stray dog.

On the way into Portomarín we saw Tiffany sitting outside an albergue, at the back of a line that was two hours long! However, many people we had managed to pass that day, there must have been pilgrims that started way before us and got to Portomarín very early. We waited in line for the two hours and finally we all got a bed.

There are around six albergues in this town, but they were all the same, packed to the brim with people. Waiting in line during the blazing sun tired me and Tiffany out so we decided after showering we would go to bed, separately. But we did end up having an hour or two in bed together while most of the albergue was out wandering the town, around 7pm. Marc was one of the people out exploring and I didn't see him again for the rest of the night. After days of walking 30km, Marc always found the energy to walk around town every single night, probably covering another 15km in doing so. He told me that Portomarín is a lovely place and that I probably should have taken an hour out to go and explore. I told him I was busy with Tiffany and he shook his head with a smile on his face.

Portomarín has the church of San Nicolás and is linked with the knights of Saint John. It had to be demolished and rebuilt, as its original site is now submerged in water.

Portomarín – Melide
40km

I woke up at 3am in the morning and couldn't get back to sleep at all. There was a French girl called Marie who was also awake in the bed next to me and we started whispering to each other that it was very hot inside the room. After a while we both decide to start walking together and at

4am when we set off, as it was already beginning to get light outside. Marc woke up at 4:30 and saw that my bed was empty, and my bag had gone, so he started walking at 5am with Mauricio. I didn't know Mauricio was in our albergue, but Marc had bumped into him while wandering around town, so they started walking together to catch up with me.

Marie was a nice girl, but she was incredibly slow at walking and when you're legs and feet are feeling good, the last thing you want to be doing is strolling. Around 13km into the morning we came to a bus stop in a place called Ventas de Narón and Marie looked at the bus times. Seeing there was a bus at 7:30, she decided to wait and was going to take the bus to Melide. She explained that she'd been walking so slowly because of the three blisters on her left foot that were very painful. I agreed she should take the bus and we said our goodbyes. What I didn't realise was today would end up being my longest day of the whole Camino at 40km, with me also going to Melide. Now I'd left Marie I really got going and enjoyed the flat, winding paths the Camino gave me. I kept my head down and kept walking at a very good pace, not stopping in the little towns I passed such as Ligonde and Eirexe (both towns have albergues and cafés). My first rest stop today was Palas de Rei and the time was 10am. I'd set off at 4am and walked 25km in six hours. I sat outside a small café and enjoyed a glass of apple juice and a cigarette before deciding to get going again. If I sat too long, I'd get comfortable and not feel like moving, so I tried not to sit outside these cafés for too long. 25km is a good day on the Camino, so if you want to stop here, rest assured there are two albergues and several hotels.

The next 15km to Melide is quite tough as there are some short, but shockingly steep, downward hills heading into San Xulian and Casanova. At around 11am the sun was already blaring, and I decided to hide in the shade for twenty minutes or so in Casanova, after finding a café while walking up a lovely country lane surrounded by rose bushes. It was only me and another gentleman in this café. He introduced himself as Paul from Australia and he began talking to me about the small town of Casanova and how it got its name. He confidently told me that Italian author Giacomo Casanova died and was buried here in 1800, and the town was named after him shortly after his passing. Now I don't claim to be a brainbox or even count myself as an intellectual, but if there is one thing I know about, it's Giacomo Casanova. I based my History GCSE coursework on him and his life. I told the man he was mistaken, and that Casanova actually died in 1798 in Dux, Bohemia (we now know it as the Czech Republic). I told him that Casanova did visit Spain in around 1767, but it was short-lived. After he landed himself in a Barcelona jail for six weeks, he headed back to Paris, where he spent most of his adult life, despite being born in Venice.

I think I shocked him, because the look of sheer disbelief on his face was priceless! I think he saw a youngster he could spin a tail to and had tried to make himself look intelligent. He told me I must be mixing him up with another Casanova and that I was mistaken. That really got my back up. When I know I'm right, I will argue until the death. Being sweaty, out of breath and feeling flustered, I couldn't be arsed with this shit, so I decided to put the conversation to bed quickly and told him:

'I 100 percent have not got him mixed up with anybody. Giacomo Casanova was born in Venice in 1725 and died in Bohemia in 1798. He was a famous author and traveller, known for wandering around Europe sleeping with as many women as he could. We even get the saying 'He/she is a Casanova' from him, as he shagged so many women, he became known throughout Europe as a womaniser. He didn't visit this part of Spain and he definitely isn't buried here. I did my History GCSE on the bloke; I know what I'm talking about, and if you want, I'll get it up on the internet for you.'

I know I bit his head off a bit, but I can't stand people that make up total bullshit to make themselves look superior to someone, and that is what he tried doing. Paul drank the last sip of his coffee, put on his rucksack, walked out of the door and didn't say another word to me.

I was around 10km to Melide now and when I started walking again, the sun was burning my skin, and it made for very uncomfortable walking. At around 1pm I walked into a town called Furelos, crossing its medieval bridge, the Ponte Velha, and taking a quick look inside its museum. From here we begin a climb to Melide through a modern suburb and end up joining a main road leading to that day's destination. I was dripping with sweat walking into Melide at 2pm and soon realised I'd walked 40km that day in ten hours. Not the quickest of paces, but I was proud of it, all the same.

I'm just glad to the day was mostly flat, and I could keep a good pace. I really began to acknowledge that day just how much my fitness had improved since that first day on the Pyrenees mountains. My legs were much stronger, and I could notice myself losing weight. I was also starting to acclimatise to the sun, and even though it might burn, it wasn't making me feel ill anymore, and the dreaded heatstroke was just a memory now. There were a lot of pilgrims walking again that day, and the first two albergues I arrived at were full, so I kept walking and found another two that were also full. I was starting to panic that there were no beds remaining, and after walking 40km I didn't want to be walking any further. I quickly got on the internet and searched for nearby hotels and found one around a kilometre out of town called the Sony Hotel. I phoned Marc and told him the situation with the albergues and that I was going to Hotel Sony. He told me he would meet me there and to try and get him and Mauricio a room as well. When I got to the hotel, I asked the manager if there were any rooms and he told me there was only one available, a small room with three single beds. I phoned Marc to tell him the good news that we could all be together for the night. Another classic example of the old saying, 'the Camino always provides.'

I paid for the room and went upstairs to wait for my friends, as they were around thirty minutes behind me. When they arrived, we all congratulated each other on today's mammoth 40km walk and took turns having a shower and changing. I decided to phone home and Marc suggests a video call so he could meet them. It was a lovely moment as I introduced Marc and Mauricio to my parents via a video call and again, just like that first night in Roncesvalles, I realised how lucky I was to be able to phone the people I love at the drop of a hat. The three of us enjoyed a meal in the hotel restaurant while Marc was also flicking through his pilgrim guidebook, explaining to us that we were now only 53km from Santiago de Compostela.

Melide dates to the tenth century and has around 10,000 inhabitants. In 1320 it obtained the Berenguel de Landoria, the right to build a castle, fortress the village and charge taxes. During a series of fights to overrule the power here, the walls of the village and the castle were destroyed. Since then, the Catholic monarchs banned the construction of any fortress in the village.

Melide – O Pedrouzo
30km

We decided we could be in Santiago within the next two days so we would walk 30km today, leaving just 23km tomorrow and more time to look around Santiago.

So today Marc, Maurizio and I headed for O Pedrouzo. At 11km in we decided to stop at a café in a place called Ribadiso, an idyllic little town on the river. Here is another great example of fate on the Camino. While I was sitting by the river I was thinking of Michelle and hoping she was having a brilliant Camino, hoping we would bump into each other again before the end of the journey. As I drank my hot chocolate and turned around to ask someone for a light for my cigarette, I saw Michelle walking towards us in the distance. I could not believe it and was so happy to see her again. As she got closer, I got out of my seat and walked towards her to give her a hug. She told me she'd been trying to catch up with us for the last few days, after someone had told her that Marc and I were around 15km in front. She'd taken a bus around the dreaded Meseta, but Marc and I had still managed to catch up and overtake her.

I can't put into words how amazing it was to see Michelle again and the four of us (Marc, Mauricio, Michelle and I) all agreed that tomorrow we would all walk into Santiago de Compostela together. We all continued walking, but soon lost track of each other as Marc stopped in a café to talk to a Canadian girl that he'd met a few days before. Maurizio and Michelle were walking quite slowly while talking, so soon I was out in front on my own, walking at a really good pace. It wasn't too hot that day and before I knew it, I was in a town called Santa Irene, just 3km away from my destination. I stopped here in a small café and waited for thirty minutes, hoping the others would catch up, but when I saw no sign of them, I decided to get to O Pedrouzo in case they'd walked past me and I hadn't realised.

I checked into an albergue at the start of town and after ninety minutes or so I started getting worried where Marc was, so I gave him a ring. He told me he hadn't seen an arrow for a while and he was entering a town called Amenal, 3km passed O Pedrouzo! Marc didn't really know how he'd managed to walk past our destination, but I bought him a bed and he walked back. Maurizio and Michelle were nowhere to be seen, and it looked like our deal to all walk into Santiago together was off. It turned out they ended up stopping in Santa Irene, the town where I'd stopped in a café to wait for them.

Marc soon arrived at the albergue and after the normal shower and change we were out exploring. We sat in one of the town's many restaurants and planned our day tomorrow, hoping to be in Santiago by 12 noon for the pilgrim Mass. Marc and I lay awake in the albergue that night talking for ages as we were the only ones in the room. We were both extremely excited to be arriving in Santiago tomorrow and couldn't believe that, after 790km, we were nearly there.

O Pedrouzo is, for many, the last stopping point before Santiago and features most amenities. It's next to the busy N-547 motorway, which leads directly to Santiago.

O Pedrouzo – Santiago de Compostela 20.1km

Today was the day Marc and I would finally walk into Santiago, and it seemed a bit surreal. During that first day on the Pyrenees I could never have imagined I would be only 20km away from Santiago, walking with a person who had now become a close friend. We really couldn't wait to get there and left around 6am, soon walking adjacent to Santiago Airport.

Kim and I had been talking through text messages the previous few days and she was due to fly home to the States that day, so I wished her a good flight. But I got a welcome shock when she told me she'd changed her flight and she would be in Santiago for the next two days. That put an extra spring in my step, so Marc and I were like speeding bullets getting to Santiago.

Soon we were in Villamaior, passing some little cafés and bars, before a gentle climb to a monument that was built to commemorate the visit of Pope John Paul II. You have a wonderful view from here and can now see the never-ending suburbs of Santiago. We passed another couple of monuments, churches and albergues during the next 8km or so, but we didn't stop at any of them, as we just needed to get to Santiago and the cathedral. We both felt it was calling us, and I loved walking through the

Santiago suburbs with the rundown, industrial buildings. After all the research I'd done, the pictures and videos I'd seen about the cathedral, I couldn't believe that in a few moments I would be there, standing in front of it.

Marc and I left the suburbs and entered the city centre, where we could see the cathedral's towers in the distance and stopped to take some photographs. We quickly marched deeper into the centre and soon found ourselves extremely close to the end. We passed through a small tunnel where a pilgrim was playing the bagpipes, so I stood and listened for a minute or so while Marc walked on alone. On leaving the tunnel I saw hundreds of pilgrims hugging and crying, all congratulating each other. I could see Marc was standing directly in the centre of the large square outside the cathedral. He towered over everyone else. I walked straight towards him without even looking at the cathedral, hugged him and told him how proud I was of him. It might not have seemed it to a lot of people, but the Camino wasn't easy for Marc mentally. He had his demons, and I know arriving in Santiago was special for him.

I slowly turned away from Marc to face the cathedral and was overwhelmed by it. I had never had a feeling like it before. I had an enormous sense of accomplishment, which I had never felt before, while being both happy and sad. I sat on my own for a while and stared at the cathedral with tears running down my cheeks. It was the first time in my life I felt like I truly belonged somewhere, and I believed that I was meant to walk the Camino. For a building to bring such a powerful, raw emotion from someone like me was strange. People might believe I was just emotional because I'd finished the walk, but I know what I felt, and that day I found a faith that will be with me forever. I'm not saying I believe in a man with a long beard, sitting in the sky controlling everything, but I do believe in fate and believe there is something more to this world than we realise. Santiago is magical and I've thought about it every single day since returning home and have been back four times. I loved sitting there, watching the hundreds of pilgrims walk to the cathedral to finish their pilgrimage.

Kim texted me to say she was coming to meet Marc and me outside the cathedral. Seeing her again was amazing, walking up to me with that big grin on her face. I'd missed her and was so happy she was still in

Santiago, so I gave her a big hug and handed her over to Marc for him to do the same.

Our attentions turned to needing a bed. Santiago was busy, and we were scared everything would be sold out. Marc told us that there was an old monastery just out of town called Seminario Menor de la Asunción and we should try there. There were 180 beds spread across four floors, and the place was really busy. On queuing, we were told we could have private, one-bedroom rooms for twenty euros, so Marc and I decided on that. We actually paid to stay two nights and each night I would sneak Kim into my room, so she didn't have to pay anything. Not a great deal of room for two people in a single bed, but we made it work.

On dropping our bags in the room, we had no time to shower and change, as we had to be back at the Cathedral for the 12am Mass. They were swinging the Botafumeiro and none of us wanted to miss it. The Botafumeiro is a giant incense burner that was originally used to fumigate the sweaty, smelly pilgrims who would enter the cathedral. Six attendants would hoist this giant incense burner off the ground, using rope, and swing it high across the cathedral.

Firstly, we stopped at the Pilgrim Office, and after a small wait we receive our Compostelas, our names are written in Latin, and I was surprised to learn my Latin name is spelled Jordannu. The certificates also told us how far we'd walked and how long it had taken us from Saint-Jean to Santiago. I have mine all framed together at home and they are a constant reminder of my greatest achievement.

We headed back to the cathedral and queued with the other pilgrims for the 12am mass, until a church attendant at the door noticed we had our Compostelas and walked us to the front of the cathedral, sitting us in perfect seats just in front of the Botafumeiro. As the giant incense began to swing, a choir started signing *Ave Maria* and everyone was taken aback by how beautiful it was. Every pilgrim was silent and in awe of what we were witnessing and it's one of my favourite memories in life. I'm never usually lost for words, but I was speechless, and it brought a tear to my eye. I think I cried more on the Camino than I did for the ten years previous.

After the swinging of the Botafumeiro, we joined the line and waited to visit the remains of St James, which are kept in the cathedral. His remains lie in a silver casket behind a glass screen and we all paid our respects, some through prayer.

We decided it was time to go back to the albergue to shower and get into some fresh clothes. We were only there two hours before deciding to go back out and explore Santiago, as we'd only seen a small part, and it's a very big city. I decided to sit opposite the cathedral again and gather my thoughts, while Marc and Kim were having a look around. I sat thinking to myself how wonderful the world is that we have things like the Camino and how lucky I was to be able to travel. I knew at that moment what I wanted out of life: I wanted to travel forever. I wanted to visit and explore as many countries as I possibly could. I realised that I had left my passport in the little bag I was carrying with me and was moving it into a safer compartment, when the little piece of paper the monks had given me back in Pamplona fell out:

'Life is a dream, realise it.'

I couldn't believe it had fallen out at that moment and took it as another sign from the Camino. I have since visited over twenty countries, mostly alone, and have walked the Camino Portuguese from Porto to Santiago three times. The second time I was lucky enough to do it with my sixty-four-year-old father. Travelling is the only thing that makes me truly happy and, hopefully, I'll die a very old man somewhere just as amazing as Santiago. I would hate to die in the little town I grew up in, that's my worst fear. When I go, I want to go doing what I love. Travelling.

I got a phone call from Marc telling me to wait at the cathedral for him as he had something amazing that he wanted to show me. I waited around for ten minutes and saw him bouncing up the street like a teenager.

'Come with me,' he said. So, I followed him down one of Santiago's narrow streets towards a coffee shop and nearly burst with excitement when I saw Kim sat with Michele and Mauricio. I really didn't think I would see them again as we'd lost them the day before, and I knew they were only staying in Santiago one night, then heading home. I was so happy they were here. They both had private hotels for the night, but it was OK, we were all together for the night, and it was fantastic.

Michele had the great idea that we should all go out tonight to a proper restaurant, no expense spared, and treat ourselves for completing the Camino. Michele picked the restaurant and we all agreed to meet there at 7pm, after we've all been back to our beds for a sleep – though Kim and I didn't do much sleeping.

Mauricio was nowhere to be seen at 7pm, so by 7:30 we'd all ordered our food and we had one of the best nights I've had. Michele brought her tablet so we could video-call Carles back in Barcelona, and it was great seeing him again. He was sad he wasn't with us, but it made him happy to know we'd finished the Camino. I also used it to videocall my parents and introduce them to my new friends. It's crazy how some of the best nights of your life are the simplest. We just sat there laughing and reminiscing like we'd all been friends fifty years, it was incredible.

Mauricio turned up as we were finishing our food and told us he'd slept late, but it didn't matter, at least he was here now. We all decided to go to a bar up the street and drink the night away together. Marc had a cider and he loved it. We knew this was our last night with Michele, as she was flying back to Canada in the morning, and it was upsetting for me to know I probably wouldn't see her again; I have so much love and respect for that woman, it's unbelievable. Michele was my Camino Mother and kept me on the straight and narrow a few times during our time together, so we raised a glass to her, and I thanked her for being part of my Camino family. Kim and I had a fair bit to drink and relied on Marc to show us the way back to the albergue, as there was no way we would have gotten back without him in our state. Even though we were drunk, Kim and I spent our last night together in the single bed and said our goodbyes before going to sleep.

The next morning, I was feeling good. Marc was already out and exploring more of Santiago but came back in time to say goodbye to Kim, as she was leaving that afternoon. The second time watching her leave wasn't as difficult as the first; I was just grateful we'd had another thirty-six hours together in Santiago that we didn't expect. When Kim left on the bus in Burgos it felt like we had unfinished business, but now it didn't. It was the right time for us to say our goodbyes. A taxi picked her up in front of the albergue and that was the last time we ever saw each other, though we do speak online now and again. We live different lives and live too far away from each other, but I'm sure I will see her again one day when I eventually visit New York.

Mauricio had managed to get a private room in our albergue for to the night, so the three of us decided to go for some food and go souvenir hunting. After a few hours of visiting the many souvenir shops and collecting our gifts for loved ones back home, we realised it was 6pm and we should probably start planning what we were doing tomorrow. None of us was ready to go home yet and we all shared the feeling that we needed to keep going. The only other option was to fly home.

The area of Santiago de Compostela was a Roman cemetery by the fourth century and was occupied by the Suebi tribes in the early fifth century, when they settled in Galicia and Portugal during the initial collapse of the Roman Empire. Medieval legend has it that the cathedral was built in the exact spot where St James's remains were found. In 1985, the city's old town was designated a UNESCO World Heritage Site. Santiago is a major city which has many shops, banks, restaurants, bars, a popular university and a population of over 200,000.

Santiago de Compostela – Vilaserio 35km

We decided to keep going. We were going to walk to Finisterre, some 87km away, which would take us an extra three days. Finisterre means 'end of the world' and it's been known as such since Roman times, as it was believed the Finisterre cliffs looking out at the Atlantic Ocean were the end of the known world. Only a small percentage of pilgrims continue to Finisterre, with most marking the end of their journey in Santiago. Marc, Mauricio and I all felt that our Camino wasn't over yet and knew we needed to continue.

So today we headed to Vilaserio, 35km away, which started with a gentle climb out of Santiago. After around thirty minutes or so you have a great view of Santiago from a small hilltop, looking back at the beautiful cathedral towering in the distance. I was sad to be leaving Santiago, but so relieved to have my boots back on and to be starting walking again. We left quite early, knowing how far we had to walk, and by 8:30 came to our first stop, a tranquil little bar with a garden that faced a river and medieval stone bridge. We all sat there for quite a while, taking in the clean air, listening to the river and enjoying the peacefulness it brought.

We didn't stop walking again until we reached Negreira, a fairly big town with a population of around 7,000 and four or five albergues. We decided to keep walking and not stop here. During this part of the walk we passed under a few archways where Spanish children had set up lemonade stands that conveniently didn't have any change, so a glass of lemonade cost me five euros. I didn't mind really; it was boiling and the best tasting lemonade I had all Camino.

Upon reaching Negreira, we bumped into an old Camino friend we hadn't seen in a long time. Bea, who had woken me and asked me to join her for drinks back in Astorga, was sitting at a little bar with some pilgrims we had yet to meet. She jumped up and gave us all a big hug, explaining she had taken a bus a few days forward and had been in Santiago two days before us. It always baffled Marc and me that when anybody caught a bus, we would still manage to catch up with them at some point, even though we walked. Maybe we were faster than we realised. Bea was walking with a Spanish nurse named Monica and an American dentist whose name I can't remember. We all had a cold drink and walked together to Vilaserio, 13km away. It was great to see Bea again and reminisce about that dreadfully hot day walking together to Foncebadón. She was such a lovely person and had an infectious personality.

Vilaserio is a really small town with not a lot of restaurants to choose from, and we found this out after showering and settling into our albergue. The 35km walk today had been great, the sun wasn't too hot, and the terrain was relatively flat. We made good time and were in the albergue by 14:30. Around 6pm we found a small restaurant down a side street and had a choice of spaghetti or fish; I think we all chose spaghetti. The thing with the small towns is that there is never a lot of choice, but I prefer that if anything. I like to keep things simple. Everyone was in bed by 9pm expect Bea and me, who chose to stay up with a bottle of white wine and talk for a few hours, leading to yet another wine hangover in the morning.

Vilaserio – Cee
40km

There is something about the ocean that brings out the real me. I can't explain it but sitting on a cliff or beach looking out at the water as far as the eye can see is magical, and somewhere where I feel at home, wherever I am in the world. I'm convinced I was a pirate or sailor in a past life and long to live near the ocean.

I knew walking a full 40km today would take me to Cee, a small town on the Atlantic. This would be the first day of my Camino that I would see the ocean. I needed it; I needed the peace that it brings me. I left before everybody else that morning, even though I had a hangover from the wine. Today was one of those days where you wake up and need to be alone. I'd had a few of them along the way, but today I had more of an urge to be alone.

At the start of today's walk you start to come down off the Galician mountains, elevate back up 400m, before a surprisingly quick decent back down to the ocean. I don't know what kept me going today, but I didn't stop, apart from a sandwich and orange juice in a town called Ponte Olveira. There was plenty of wind today, the sun wasn't as vicious as usual, and I could smell the ocean in the air which kept me surging forward. It took me around nine hours to walk the 40km today, leaving at 6am and getting into Cee at around 3pm. Descending into Cee and finally seeing the ocean in the distance made me stop in my tracks and appreciate a sight I hadn't seen in weeks. I had a smile on my face and practically ran the last 2km.

As I was the first to enter Cee, I went straight to an albergue just around the corner from the small harbour. I phoned Marc to tell him I had arrived and picked six beds for us all in a quiet corner of the albergue. Turned out it was only us sleeping there that night. A few hours later, Marc, Mauricio, Bea and her two friends turned up and it was nice to see them. I'd been on my own all day, like I wanted, but now I needed human interaction again. A lot of the group fell asleep when they got in, but Marc and I decided to sit outside a bar on the harbour with a beer. I sat there for about two hours just staring at the water, breathing in the fresh, clean air and loving every second of it.

Around 7pm we all went for a big dinner in a restaurant facing the sea and had a smashing night. Mauricio, Bea and I all had more beers than we should have, and again, I can't remember getting back to the albergue. During the evening, one of the women Bea was walking with began to really annoy us all. She was a dentist from Texas and was so loud it became embarrassing to have other diners shaking their heads in our direction. Marc, Mauricio and I spoke privately about giving them the slip in the morning and walking the short 17km to Finisterre together.

Cee has a population of 8,000 and, like a lot of Galician villages in this area, was largely destroyed by Napoleon and his army back in the early 1800s.

Cee – Finisterre
17km

The three of us woke at 7:30 and started to get ready to leave. Bea was still waiting in the albergue and informed us the annoying dentist and the lovely Monica had woken before us and left. The four of us left together and spent the first part of the walk going over the past few weeks, reminiscing about the good times, bad times and how it had changed us.

Bea would be leaving us in Finisterre and although it was sad, it was great to see her and get to walk with her again. When the others decided to stop at a small café soon after leaving, I decided I wanted to walk into Finisterre alone and kept on walking. Today was such a glorious walk through woodland, before an incline to a busy road and into Finisterre. When leaving the woodland, you can see the Atlantic Ocean in all its glory, with its glistening waters and golden beach.

I was soon at the bottom of the incline and decided to walk along the sand, instead of next to the road. The walk across the beach should have taken me fifteen minutes, but I made it last an hour, sampling a few beers in the beach bars and admiring the view. After a while I noticed a lot of pilgrims pass and decided to go and find an albergue before everywhere got full, and I was just in time. I found a room in a private hostel up a small side street and settled in, getting showered and waiting for Marc.

Soon after, I received a phone call from Marc asking where my albergue was as he couldn't find anywhere to stay. People stay in Finisterre for two or three days, so the beds that remain are booked up quickly. I told him where I was staying, and he came over to try and find a room. The little old woman in charge told Marc she only had two rooms and they were both occupied, but she might be able to sort out something else for him. The owner's sister soon came in and told Marc he could sleep in the spare bedroom at her home, the Camino providing once again.

Marc's room was just up the road from me, so forty minutes later we decided to go and meet Mauricio, who'd found a hotel room, and we all headed for the beach. We agreed to not visit the lighthouse and cliffs of Finisterre until around 21:30, so we could all watch the sunset together. Hundreds of people turn up every night to watch it and you have to be a bit early to get a good spot.

On the beach, Mauricio and I started talking to a few other pilgrims and decided to join them in a game of beach football while Marc looked around Finisterre. We were on opposite teams and Mauricio and I enjoyed the challenge of tackling each other and trying to trip each other up… That's when we heard the crunch.

We'd both tried to kick the ball at the same time but missed, and instead kicked each other's foot. I heard and felt his big toe break as it hit my foot, then the limping and profanities started. He was in a lot of pain and, being his big toe, I knew straight away this was the end of his Camino. Marc and I walked him to a pharmacy where they strapped up the broken toe and told him to rest.

Mauricio was gutted that this was the end, but also very proud of himself and rightly so. He'd walked over 600 miles and had every right to be proud of what he'd achieved. Not walking to Muxia tomorrow wasn't the end of the world. After showering to get all the sand off us, we decided to go for food before going to the cliffs to watch the sunset. Finisterre, being on the coast, is famous for its seafood, and we all shared a big plate of *pulpo* and had a beer each.

We left the restaurant after an hour or so and decided to walk the 4km uphill to the cliffs of Finisterre and watch the sunset. The walk took us a bit longer than usual as we waited for the injured Mauricio to hobble up the hill, but we found a brilliant spot. On entering the cliffs, we saw another famous sign of the Camino and one that felt very surreal to see…

The 0.00km sign. Now we had truly finished!!!

On my second day in Roncesvalles, I walked past the 'Santiago de Compostela 790km' sign. Now, at the top of the cliffs in Finisterre, I had finally finished. I crossed the border into Spain more than forty days ago and literally walked across the country until I physically couldn't take one more step, without falling off the cliffs and into the Atlantic Ocean. That was an incredible feeling!

Bea was also on the cliffs and the four of us sat down together, watching the sun go down over the Atlantic Ocean. Pilgrims near us were burning their boots and some of their clothes on the cliffs, an old tradition to mark the end of one's pilgrimage. The sunset was astonishing. The sky lights up like an orange fireball before slowly melting away behind the never-ending ocean. Hundreds of pilgrims then applauded, cheered and congratulated each other on what was a gruelling, life-changing pilgrimage across Spain. The bond pilgrims form with each other is unbreakable. You might not know each other, but when you meet on the road you help each other. You talk, you share secrets, and you live in each other's lives, even if it's only for an hour. Then at the end, when it's over, you say goodbye and never see each other again. But you'll always have that bond. You've walked over 600 miles together; you can never forget something like that.

After coming down from the cliffs and back to the centre of Finisterre, Marc and I said our final goodbyes to Mauricio and Bea. It was sad, especially saying goodbye to Mauricio as he couldn't walk any further. I lost contact with Bea after the Camino and she isn't on social media, but it would be lovely to speak to her again.

Marc and I sat outside a café at around 11pm, both sad that we had to say goodbye to more friends. But we both agreed that our Camino wasn't quite over yet. We agreed on another day of walking, to finish the Camino our way.

Finisterre is a busy fishing town with a population of around 6,000, but that number increases massively during the summer due to pilgrims and tourists. The famed lighthouse of Finisterre is now a museum but is still used for tracking purposes by ships.

Finisterre – Muxia
29km

Marc and I had both seen the movie *The Way* before coming on the Camino. In the movie, Martin Sheen doesn't visit Finisterre after Santiago, he walks straight to Muxia. His character in the movie walks the Camino after his son dies on the Pyrenees mountains, also on the pilgrimage. He stands on the rocks of Muxia and scatters his son's ashes into the ocean after completing the Camino. Marc and I had wanted to visit Muxia since the start of the Camino, so we decided we'd have one more day on the road and walk the 29km. Again, an even smaller number of pilgrims decided to walk to Muxia, so we were alone today.

The walk is delightful, with forest paths, farm tracks and views of the ocean appearing every so often through the trees. We stopped in a place called Lires and had a quick drink and something to eat before continuing, but soon came down off the mountain and into Muxia, passing across sand and rocks before taking the main road into the town. We decided to head straight to the ocean rocks where Martin Sheen stood during the movie, walking past the small church that stands guard at the foot of the water. I stood where Martin Sheen scattered the ashes and stared out at the ocean, knowing that my Camino was finally over. I sat on the rocks, letting the water crash over my legs and, like I did in Santiago, had a great sense of accomplishment.

Over 600 miles after leaving Saint-Jean-Pied-de-Port, I had finished.

Reflection

It was absolutely soul destroying when I lost my passport on the first day of walking and had to turn back, but it turned out to be the best thing that happened to me. If I hadn't gone back, I might never have met Marc, Kim, Mauricio and Michele. There were plenty more people I had the pleasure of meeting, but without meeting them, I can't imagine what my Camino would have been like. It's not always about the destination, it's about who you get there with, and I couldn't have wished for better people. The Camino changed my whole outlook on life, but I also have Marc to thank for that. Marc and the Camino changed me as a person, and I also know we did the same for him. It's funny, because my parents are my heroes and your parents are usually the people to shape your life, but for me it was Marc and I owe him so much. Every bit of anger, stubbornness, courage and strength I have, I get from my father. The love, creativity, compassion and happiness I get from my mother. Yet Marc has had the biggest impact on me. At a time when I needed hope and guidance, he gave me some and was the friend I had always been missing. I love you, Marc, and thank you, for everything.

One thing I realised about the Camino is that you never reach your destination. You can reach Santiago, Finisterre or Muxia, but it's only when you get home that you realise that the Camino is never finished. You can be walking down the street back home and see a yellow arrow, and it will remind you of the Camino. It is always on your mind and you find yourself talking about it constantly, to whoever will listen.

It's never finished.
It will always be there.
It will always bring you back.

A lot of people walk the Camino looking for answers, but there's no need. The answers will find you when you least expect it.

Life has a funny way of sorting itself out and when you strip back all the shit, you realise that it's still a remarkable, amazing world out there. Bad things have to happen to make us appreciate the good. Rainbows after storms and sunrises after darkness. If you trust that life has a plan for you, you're halfway there. Life is a unique beauty. There is always something magic, there is always something new.

Some of us were just born to run away,
to see the world from the other side.

I came on the Camino to find myself, but I already knew who I was.
I just found a better version.

See you all soon… Somewhere Along the Way.

Acknowledgements

Marc Geboers – My true best friend. I owe half of this book to you, as without your memory and photographs, I would have been stuffed. The kindest, most patient, caring, gentle soul I have ever met.
I'm a better person for knowing you.
We changed each other. Fate brought us together.

Kim Simek – Made me realise I still had a heart. You deserve happiness and I pray you find it. A part of me will always be in Spain with you.

Michele Catalano – My Camino mother. Kept me grounded and told me what I needed to hear, good or bad. One of life's kindest.

My parents – For listening to me ramble on about this book for the last five years. For encouraging me to keep going. I love you both.

John Lewis – Thanks for saving the book when my laptop broke. If it weren't for you recovering it, there would be no book.

To everybody I met along the Camino – Thank you for being part of this book and letting me tell our story. I miss you all. Thank you for being part of the amazing memories I cherish.

Contact details

Email: jordanjoneslufc@hotmail.co.uk
Phone: +447732068680

Printed in Great Britain
by Amazon